STOCHASTIC VOLATILITY MODELING

Trading Strategies with Python

Hayden Van Der Post
Vincent Bisette

Reactive Publishing

CONTENTS

PREFACE

In the ever-evolving world of financial markets, the quest for robust trading strategies that can adapt to market uncertainties remains paramount. 'Stochastic Volatility Modeling: Trading Strategies with Python' emerges as a beacon for professionals poised on the cutting edge of quantitative finance, seeking to harness the complex dynamics of market volatility. This book is crafted for those who have ventured into quantitative finance and are now ready to elevate their skills by intertwining theory with practical, real-world applications.

With the surge of interest in stochastic models and their application in financial markets, the need for a comprehensive guide that navigates through the landscapes of volatility modeling has never been more critical. Whether you found solace in the pages of introductory quant finance materials or you've been at the helm of developing basic trading strategies, this book is designed to propel you into the next level of your professional journey.

Our journey begins at the intersection of theory and practice, where sophisticated models of stochastic volatility are not merely discussed but are also implemented. Through the lens of Python, a language that has become synonymous with computational finance, we delve deep into not only the "how" but also the "why" behind model selection, calibration, and implementation into trading strategies.

This book is not a mere continuation of what has been; it is a leap into what can be. It targets individuals who have previously encountered the basics of quantitative finance, perhaps through top-selling books in the arena, but are now seeking more , sophisticated techniques and applications. Our readers are professionals who aspire to not just understand, but also to apply advanced stochastic volatility models in crafting innovative trading strategies.

In 'Stochastic Volatility Modeling: Trading Strategies with Python,' we do more than explore cutting-edge models; we break down these complex concepts into digestible sections, accompanied by practical examples that illuminate the path from theory to application. Each chapter is framed to build upon the previous, ensuring a gradual elevation of the reader's expertise, culminating in the mastery of advanced trading strategies empowered by stochastic volatility models.

As you embark on this journey, remember that the path to mastery is not linear. It is a journey fraught with challenges, requiring perseverance, creativity, and the willingness to explore uncharted territories. This book provides the map and the tools, but the journey will be uniquely yours.

Welcome to an exploration that promises to deepen your understanding, enhance your skill set, and ultimately, empower you to leverage stochastic volatility in crafting sophisticated trading strategies that resonate with the complexity of today's financial markets.

May this book serve not only as your guide but also as your inspiration to push beyond the boundaries of traditional finance, embracing the volatility that shapes our markets and our world.

Let's begin.

CHAPTER 1: FOUNDATIONS OF STOCHASTIC VOLATILITY MODELS

Volatility, in the financial lexicon, is a multifaceted concept that serves as the heartbeat of the markets, indicating both opportunities and risks. It is the statistical measure of the dispersion of returns for a given security or market index, encompassing the sways and swells of prices over time. Understanding volatility is crucial for anyone venturing into stochastic volatility modeling, as it constitutes the foundation upon which these models are constructed and calibrated.

volatility is about uncertainty. It is a reflection of the degree to which the price of an asset varies over a specific period. High volatility indicates that the price of the asset can change dramatically over a short time period in either direction, signaling a higher degree of risk. Conversely, low volatility denotes lesser price movement and, ostensibly, lower risk. However, it is critical to acknowledge that in the realms of finance and investment, 'risk' is not merely a threat but also harbors potential for reward.

Volatility is typically measured by the standard deviation of the returns of an asset over a set period. This mathematical approach offers a clear, quantifiable insight into the variability of an asset's price. Another commonly used metric is the variance, the square of the standard deviation, which also serves to measure price dispersion. These metrics provide the scaffolding for more sophisticated volatility models and are indispensable tools in the quant's toolkit.

Volatility bifurcates into historical (or realized) volatility and implied volatility. Historical volatility measures the fluctuations of an asset's price in the past, offering a backward-looking perspective. It is calculated by determining the standard deviation of the historical returns of the asset.

In contrast, implied volatility looks to the future. It is derived from the price of an asset's options, reflecting the market's expectation of how volatile the asset will be over the life of the option. Implied volatility is profoundly influential in the pricing of options and is a pivotal component in the Black-Scholes model, among other pricing models.

The modeling of volatility is not a pursuit of precision in predicting exact future prices but rather an endeavor to understand the nature of their movement and distribution. In this context, stochastic processes, which are mathematical models designed to predict the probability distribution of potential future states of a system, become invaluable. They allow for the modeling of volatility as a dynamic, evolving entity, influenced by a confluence of factors and subject to change over time.

Two phenomena closely associated with financial market volatility are volatility clustering and mean reversion. Volatility clustering suggests that large price changes tend to be followed by more large changes, of either sign, and small changes tend to be followed by small changes. This observation is a cornerstone in constructing models that anticipate the clustering of volatility.

On the other hand, mean reversion posits that volatility will tend to return to an average level over time. This principle is crucial in modeling long-term market behaviors, offering a counterbalance to the short-term prediction of volatility clustering.

Understanding volatility is akin to decrypting the language of the markets. It requires a blend of mathematical rigor, statistical insight, and a nuanced appreciation of market psychology. As we journey further into stochastic volatility models, keeping the fundamental concepts of volatility in sharp focus will illuminate the path. The exploration of stochastic processes, historical versus implied volatility, and phenomena like volatility clustering and mean reversion, not only enriches this understanding but also empowers the development of sophisticated models capable of navigating the turbulent waters of financial markets.

Volatility is not merely a statistical measure; it is the lifeblood of the financial markets, driving decision-making and strategy for investors, traders, and portfolio managers. Its importance cannot be overstated—it is a proxy for risk, and understanding it is fundamental to achieving return objectives while managing exposure to loss.

1. Risk Assessment: Volatility is a critical component in the assessment of risk. High volatility signifies higher risk, as the asset price is more likely to experience significant changes over a short period. Conversely, low volatility suggests a more

stable asset, with less potential for rapid change. Investors use this information to align their portfolio with their risk tolerance and investment horizon.

2. Pricing of Financial Instruments: The valuation of options and other derivatives is inherently linked to volatility. Models like Black-Scholes rely heavily on volatility as a key input, influencing the premium paid or received for these financial instruments. The implied volatility, gleaned from option prices, offers insight into market sentiment and expectations of future price movements.

3. Strategic Trading and Hedging: Traders leverage volatility to identify profit opportunities, employing strategies that capitalize on predicted market movements. Additionally, volatility is a cornerstone in hedging techniques, where positions are taken to mitigate potential losses due to adverse price movements in other investments.

4. Portfolio Diversification: Understanding the volatility of assets enables the construction of diversified portfolios that aim to optimize the risk-return profile. By combining assets with differing volatilities, investors can potentially reduce the overall volatility of their portfolio, mitigating risk while pursuing desired returns.

Beyond its role in risk assessment and pricing, volatility also functions as a broader market indicator. Periods of increased volatility often signal market uncertainty or fear, potentially indicative of economic or geopolitical turmoil. Conversely, low volatility periods might suggest market complacency or stability. Thus, volatility indices, such as the VIX (often referred to as the "fear index"), serve as vital gauges of market sentiment and risk appetite.

It's crucial to recognize that volatility is not static; it fluctuates over time in response to market dynamics, economic data, geopolitical events, and changes in investor behavior. This dynamic nature of volatility underscores the need for continuous monitoring and adjustment of strategies by market participants.

The implications of volatility extend beyond financial markets. Economic decision-making, corporate finance strategies, and even regulatory policies are influenced by an understanding of volatility and its effects. For businesses, volatility in commodity prices, exchange rates, and interest rates can have direct impacts on costs, pricing, and profitability, necessitating sophisticated risk management strategies.

The definition and importance of volatility in financial markets encompass a broad spectrum of considerations, from its foundational role in pricing and risk assessment to its influence on strategic decision-making and market sentiment. As we continue to explore stochastic volatility models, keeping the pivotal role of volatility in financial markets in sharp focus will be essential. It is the prism through which we can better understand market dynamics, develop robust trading strategies, and ultimately, navigate the complexities of modern financial markets with greater acumen and confidence.

Historical Volatility vs. Implied Volatility

In the discourse on financial market volatility, two concepts stand prominently: historical volatility and implied volatility. Both play critical roles in financial analysis, trading strategies, and risk management, yet they diverge significantly in their computation, interpretation, and application. Understanding the nuances between them is paramount for anyone looking to navigate the financial markets with acumen.

Historical volatility, often referred to as realized volatility, pertains to the actual fluctuation in the price of an asset over a specific past period. It is calculated by analyzing the standard deviation of the logarithmic returns of the asset, typically on a daily basis, over this period. By doing so, historical volatility offers a gauge of how much the asset price has varied around its mean in the past.

1. Quantitative Insight: Historical volatility provides a quantitative measure of past market behavior. It is empirical, grounded in actual observed data, making it a factual representation of an asset's risk profile as experienced over the selected timeframe.

2. Lagging Indicator: As a measure based on past data, historical volatility is inherently a lagging indicator. It offers insights into what has occurred but lacks the capacity to predict future volatility or market movements.

3. Strategic Application: Investors and analysts use historical volatility to assess risk, inform asset allocation, and develop strategies based on past market behavior. It is also vital in benchmarking the performance of volatility forecasting models.

Implied volatility, in contrast, is a forward-looking measure derived from the pricing of options or other derivatives. It reflects the market's expectation of future volatility of the underlying asset until the option's expiration. Unlike historical volatility, implied volatility is not calculated from past price data but is inferred from the market price of the derivative itself.

1. Expectation of Future Volatility: Implied volatility represents the market consensus on how volatile an asset is expected to be in the future. It is a projection, subject to market sentiments, events, and participant behaviors.

2. Dynamic and Responsive: Implied volatility is highly responsive to market dynamics, capable of swift adjustments based on new information, making it a real-time indicator of market sentiment and perceived risk.

3. Pricing and Strategy: It plays a central role in the pricing of options and other derivatives. Traders and portfolio managers use implied volatility to identify potential trading opportunities, hedge against market movements, and gauge the market's risk expectation.

The relationship and disparities between historical and implied volatility offer a rich tapestry for analysis and strategy formulation in financial markets. While historical volatility serves as a solid foundation, providing a sense of how volatile an asset has been, implied volatility offers a glimpse into the market's future expectations. This dichotomy forms the basis for various trading strategies, such as volatility arbitrage, where discrepancies between an asset's historical and implied volatility may signal opportunities.

Moreover, the comparison between the two can reveal market sentiments. A higher implied volatility compared to historical volatility might suggest that traders expect more significant fluctuations in the future, possibly due to impending news or events. Conversely, lower implied volatility might indicate a period of consolidation or reduced uncertainty.

The contrasting yet complementary nature of historical and implied volatility sketches a nuanced portrait of market dynamics. For practitioners in the financial markets, mastering the understanding and application of both measures is indispensable. Historical volatility offers a rearview mirror, reflecting the path traveled, while implied volatility casts its gaze forward, anticipating the road ahead. Together, they form an essential toolkit for anyone engaged in the art and science of market analysis, trading, and risk management, providing critical insights that navigate the churning seas of financial markets with greater precision and foresight.

The Concept of Stochastic Processes in Financial Modeling

1. Defining Stochastic Processes: a stochastic process is a mathematical object defined as a collection of random variables, representing the evolution of some system over time in a probabilistic manner. In financial markets, this 'system' often refers to the price movements of assets or interest rates, where the future state is uncertain and can be described only in terms of probabilities.

2. Classification and Examples: Stochastic processes are classified into various types based on their state space, index set, and evolution properties. Notable examples include Brownian motion, which models the continuous and random movement of asset prices, and Poisson processes, typically used for modeling the count of discrete events over time, such

as jumps in an asset's price.

3. Markov Chains and Property: A significant subclass of stochastic processes is the Markov chain, characterized by the Markov property. This property posits that the future state of a process depends only on the current state, not on the sequence of events that preceded it. Markov chains are invaluable in algorithmic trading and risk management, offering a simplified yet powerful approach to modeling financial systems.

4. Option Pricing Models: The most celebrated application of stochastic processes in finance is perhaps in the Black-Scholes-Merton model and its extensions for option pricing. These models utilize the concept of geometric Brownian motion to describe the dynamics of stock prices, laying the groundwork for a theoretical framework for valuing options.

5. Interest Rate Models: Stochastic processes are also foundational in modeling interest rates, crucial for fixed income markets. Models such as the Vasicek and Cox-Ingersoll-Ross models describe the evolution of interest rates using stochastic differential equations, enabling analysts to price bonds, interest rate derivatives, and manage interest rate risk.

6. Portfolio Optimization and Risk Management: The application of stochastic processes extends beyond pricing to encompass portfolio optimization and risk management. Techniques such as Monte Carlo simulation, grounded in stochastic process theory, allow for the exploration of thousands of possible future scenarios, aiding in portfolio selection and risk assessment.

modeling with stochastic processes lies the domain of stochastic differential equations (SDEs). These equations govern the behavior of stochastic processes and are pivotal in translating the theory into practical models for financial analysis. Solving SDEs involves numerical methods and simulation techniques, requiring a deep understanding of both mathematics and the computational tools at hand.

7. Ito Calculus: A cornerstone in the study of SDEs is Ito calculus, which extends classical calculus to accommodate stochastic integration and differentiation. It provides the mathematical framework for modeling the random motion of asset prices and interest rates.

8. Simulation Techniques: Numerical solutions to SDEs, such as the Euler-Maruyama and Milstein methods, enable the simulation of stochastic processes. These techniques are instrumental in option pricing, risk management, and developing trading strategies.

From Constant Volatility Models to Stochastic Volatility Models

In the early days, financial models were built on the simplifying assumption of constant volatility. The most iconic of these is the Black-Scholes model, which revolutionized option pricing by assuming that the volatility of the underlying asset is a constant over the life of the option. This assumption enabled the derivation of a closed-form solution for option pricing, offering clarity and precision that was groundbreaking at the time.

However, the constant volatility assumption is akin to navigating a stormy sea assuming calm waters—the model's predictions often diverged from real market behavior, especially in times of financial stress. The 1987 market crash, among other events, exposed the limitations of constant volatility models, highlighting their inability to account for the dynamic nature of market volatility.

Recognizing the limitations of constant volatility models, the financial academia and industry began to explore more sophisticated approaches that could capture the dynamic nature of market volatility. This led to the development of stochastic volatility (SV) models, where volatility is no longer a static parameter but a variable that evolves over time according to its stochastic process.

Among the first to challenge the constant volatility paradigm were the Heston model and the SABR (Stochastic Alpha, Beta, Rho) model. The Heston model, in particular, became a cornerstone in this new era, offering a closed-form solution for European options under stochastic volatility. It models volatility as a mean-reverting process, capturing the volatility smile—a phenomenon that constant volatility models could not explain.

Stochastic volatility models introduced a level of realism and flexibility previously unseen. By allowing volatility to fluctuate, these models could more accurately mirror the empirical observations of market behavior, including the leptokurtic nature of asset returns and the appearance of volatility clustering. This enhanced realism significantly improved the pricing of derivatives, particularly for long-dated options where the assumption of constant volatility was most problematic.

The shift towards stochastic volatility models demanded a reevaluation of the mathematical and computational tools at the disposal of financial modelers. Solving SV models often involves complex numerical methods, including Monte Carlo simulations and finite difference methods, due to the absence of analytical solutions for most exotic options. This complexity necessitated advancements in computational finance, ushering in a new age of high-powered computing and sophisticated algorithms capable of handling the demands of SV modeling.

Despite their superiority in capturing market dynamics, stochastic volatility models are not without their challenges. The calibration of these models to market data can be a computationally intensive process, often requiring sophisticated optimization techniques to estimate model parameters accurately.

The quest for more accurate models led to the development of hybrid approaches that combine stochastic volatility with jumps and other mechanisms to capture sudden market movements. These models aim to provide a more comprehensive framework for understanding the multifaceted nature of financial markets.

The transition from constant volatility models to stochastic volatility models represents a significant leap forward in financial modeling. It embodies the industry's ongoing pursuit of accuracy and depth in understanding market dynamics. As we continue to explore the frontiers of financial mathematics, stochastic volatility models serve as a beacon, guiding us toward a more nuanced comprehension of the markets. The journey from simplicity to complexity, from assumption to realism, reflects the evolving nature of financial modeling—an odyssey that promises more insights and innovations in the years to come.

The Limitations of the Black-Scholes Model and the Need for Stochastic Volatility

The Black-Scholes model, since its inception in 1973, has served as the cornerstone of financial derivatives pricing. Its elegance lies in its simplicity—providing a closed-form solution for the pricing of European options under the assumption of constant volatility. However, the financial markets, in their inherent complexity and dynamism, began to reveal the cracks in this foundational framework, prompting a reassessment of its underlying assumptions.

The most critical limitation of the Black-Scholes model arises from its assumption that the volatility of the underlying asset remains constant over the option's life. This assumption, while simplifying the mathematical treatment, diverges significantly from empirical observations. Real-world markets are characterized by periods of tranquility punctuated by bouts of high volatility, a phenomenon starkly at odds with the notion of constant volatility.

The 1987 market crash, among other turbulent events, served as a stark reminder of the Black-Scholes model's limitations. The model's inability to account for the leptokurtic nature of asset returns—where extreme movements are more common than predicted by a normal distribution—resulted in systematic mispricings of options, particularly those far from expiration. This misalignment with market realities underscored the need for a model that can adapt to the shifting sands of market volatility.

The recognition of these limitations catalyzed the development of stochastic volatility (SV) models, wherein volatility is not a constant but a variable that changes over time following its own stochastic process. This approach mirrors the observed market behavior more closely, incorporating the fact that volatility is not static but dynamic, influenced by myriad factors ranging from macroeconomic announcements to market sentiment.

By allowing volatility to be stochastic, SV models offer a more nuanced view of market dynamics. They provide a framework for understanding volatility smiles and smirks—phenomena where implied volatility differs across strike prices and maturities, something the Black-Scholes model could not explain. This capability makes SV models invaluable for pricing complex derivatives and managing the risks inherent in volatile markets.

The shift from the Black-Scholes framework to stochastic volatility models is not without challenges. The introduction of stochastic volatility complicates the pricing of options, often precluding analytical solutions and necessitating numerical methods such as Monte Carlo simulations and finite difference methods for solution approximation.

The computational intensity of these methods highlights the need for advanced computational resources and algorithms. It demands a delicate balance between accuracy and computational feasibility, pushing the boundaries of both financial mathematics and computational finance.

Further, the calibration of SV models to market data presents its own set of challenges. Estimating the parameters of stochastic processes governing volatility requires sophisticated statistical techniques and a deep understanding of market dynamics, underscoring the complexity of implementing SV models.

The limitations of the Black-Scholes model have illuminated the path towards more sophisticated approaches to financial modeling. The transition to stochastic volatility models marks a pivotal evolution in the quest to encapsulate the realities of market dynamics. This journey, from the simplistic assumptions of constant volatility to the complex stochasticity of market behavior, reflects a broader theme in financial modeling: the continuous strive for models that can more faithfully mirror the multifaceted nature of financial markets. As we venture further into this realm, the need for innovation, flexibility, and a deep understanding of market intricacies remains paramount, guiding our pursuit of models that resonate with the nuanced rhythm of market volatility.

Overview of Major Stochastic Volatility Models: Heston and SABR at the Forefront

Conceived by Steven Heston in 1993, the Heston model introduced a revolutionary approach to modeling volatility by allowing it to follow a stochastic process characterized by mean reversion. The model is built on the premise that volatility is not a static entity but evolves over time, influenced by market forces and reverting to a long-term mean. Mathematically, it is delineated by a system of stochastic differential equations (SDEs) that describe the dynamics of both the asset price and its variance.

The Heston model is the Cox-Ingersoll-Ross (CIR) process, governing the evolution of variance. This process ensures the positiveness of the variance, a crucial aspect that aligns with empirical market observations. The model is particularly esteemed for its analytical tractability in option pricing, providing a semi-closed form solution for European call and put options.

The Heston model's ability to capture the volatility smile—a graphical representation of how implied volatility varies with both strike price and expiration—has cemented its utility in risk management and derivative pricing. Its parameters reflect key market dynamics, such as the level of mean reversion, the volatility of volatility, and the correlation between asset returns and volatility, offering deep insights into market sentiment and investor behavior.

The SABR model, developed by Patrick Hagan et al. in 2002, represents a further advancement in stochastic volatility modeling. It focuses on capturing the dynamics of the volatility smile in the derivatives market, making it particularly relevant for interest rate derivatives. The model assumes that both the asset price and its volatility follow stochastic processes, with volatility itself following a lognormal distribution.

One of the SABR model's distinguishing features is its flexibility in fitting different shapes of volatility smiles, using a minimal set of parameters. It offers an asymptotic solution for implied volatility, allowing for efficient and accurate pricing of European options without resorting to computationally intensive numerical methods.

Despite its strengths, the SABR model requires careful calibration to market data, a task that can be challenging in markets with sparse or noisy data. Moreover, its assumption of a lognormal distribution for volatility may not capture extreme market conditions as accurately as some alternative distributions.

Both the Heston and SABR models have significantly enriched the toolbox of quantitative finance, each with its unique strengths and areas of application. The choice between these models often hinges on the specific market conditions, the type of derivatives being priced, and the computational resources available.

The Heston model's analytical solutions make it desirable for markets where computational efficiency and accuracy are paramount. Conversely, the SABR model's flexibility in fitting volatility smiles makes it invaluable in markets where the shape of the smile is complex and evolving.

While the Heston and SABR models dominate the discussion on stochastic volatility, the quest for more comprehensive and adaptable models continues. The development of models that can capture the multifaceted aspects of market behavior, from jumps in asset prices to the impact of macroeconomic events on volatility, remains an active area of research.

The exploration of stochastic volatility models like Heston and SABR represents just one chapter in the ongoing saga of financial modeling. As markets evolve, so too must our models, tools, and techniques. The continuous interplay between mathematical innovation and empirical observation stands at the core of quantitative finance, driving forward our understanding of the complex world of financial markets.

Mathematical Preliminaries: The Bedrock of Stochastic Volatility Models

At the center of stochastic volatility models lies the concept of stochastic processes. These mathematical objects are used to model systems that evolve over time under the influence of random factors. In the financial markets, this randomness can stem from a multitude of sources, such as macroeconomic indicators, market sentiment, or geopolitical events.

Itō's Calculus and Stochastic Differential Equations (SDEs): Itō's calculus introduces a framework for integrating functions over stochastic processes, laying the groundwork for the formulation of stochastic differential equations. These SDEs are pivotal in modeling the erratic movements of financial assets and their volatility. The quintessential Itō's Lemma provides a method to calculate the differential of a function of a stochastic process, a cornerstone in the derivation of many stochastic volatility models.

Random Variables and Distributions: Understanding stochastic volatility requires a deep dive into the behavior of random variables and their probability distributions. These distributions characterize the likelihood of various outcomes, from asset prices to market volatility, and are essential in assessing risks and predicting future movements.

Measure Theory and Martingales: A more sophisticated layer of probability theory involves measure theory and martingales. Measure theory provides a rigorous framework for defining probabilities on infinite sets, crucial for continuous-time models. Martingales, on the other hand, are types of stochastic processes that model fair games, embodying the idea of "no free lunch" in financial markets. The martingale property is a fundamental assumption in many pricing models, ensuring that current prices are the best predictors of future prices, devoid of arbitrage opportunities.

Solving SDEs Numerically: While some stochastic volatility models offer closed-form solutions, many require numerical methods for their solutions. Techniques such as the Euler-Maruyama method allow for the approximation of solutions to SDEs, facilitating the simulation of asset paths and the valuation of complex derivatives.

Monte Carlo Simulations: Among the most powerful tools in the quantitative finance arsenal are Monte Carlo simulations. These computational algorithms rely on repeated random sampling to obtain numerical results, enabling the valuation of derivatives under stochastic volatility models by simulating a multitude of potential market scenarios.

Vectors and Matrices in Financial Modeling: Linear algebra, with its focus on vectors, matrices, and linear transformations, is indispensable in structuring and solving financial models. Covariance matrices, for instance, capture the relationships between different asset returns, informing portfolio optimization and risk management strategies.

Eigenvalues and Eigenvectors: The concepts of eigenvalues and eigenvectors play a critical role in assessing the stability of financial systems and in pattern recognition within financial time series, providing insights into the principal components driving market movements.

Basic Concepts in Stochastic Calculus Necessary for Understanding Stochastic Volatility Models

In stochastic calculus lies the Wiener process, also known as Brownian motion. Named after Norbert Wiener, it represents a continuous-time stochastic process that models the random motion observed in phenomena such as the diffusion of particles or the fluctuation of stock prices. Key characteristics of the Wiener process include its start at zero, continuous yet nowhere differentiable paths, and having independent increments with mean zero and variance proportional to the time elapsed.

The Wiener process serves as the primary building block for modeling asset price dynamics in the Black-Scholes model and various stochastic volatility models. Its unpredictable path mirrors the erratic behavior of asset prices over time, providing a mathematical foundation for incorporating randomness into financial models.

Itō's Lemma plays a central role in stochastic calculus, much like the chain rule in traditional calculus. It allows for the differentiation of functions of a stochastic process, providing a way to calculate the change in a dependent variable when an independent variable undergoes a stochastic change. This lemma is crucial for deriving the dynamics of complex financial models involving stochastic processes.

Itō's Lemma underpins the mathematical framework for stochastic volatility models, enabling the derivation of partial differential equations that describe the evolution of asset prices and volatilities over time. It serves as the essential tool for connecting stochastic processes with practical financial modeling.

Stochastic differential equations extend the concept of ordinary differential equations to include terms that incorporate randomness, typically represented by a Wiener process. These equations are instrumental in formulating the behavior of financial assets and their volatilities under the influence of random market forces.

While exact solutions to SDEs are rare, understanding their structure and properties is crucial for applying numerical methods and simulations, such as Monte Carlo methods, to solve them. The ability to work with SDEs is fundamental for anyone involved in stochastic volatility modeling, as it directly impacts the development and calibration of models.

A martingale is a type of stochastic process that models a fair game, where the expected value of future observations equals the present observation, given all past information. In finance, the martingale property implies that current asset prices reflect all known information, thereby embodying the concept of efficient markets.

Measure theory provides the mathematical underpinnings for changing probability measures, a technique used in risk-neutral valuation. This approach simplifies the pricing of derivatives by assuming a world where investors are indifferent to risk, allowing for the use of martingales in calculating the expected values of future payoffs.

Stochastic calculus offers a gateway into the sophisticated world of financial modeling, particularly in understanding and applying stochastic volatility models. By grasping these basic concepts, from the erratic paths of the Wiener process to the transformative Itō's Lemma, financial practitioners equip themselves with the tools necessary to navigate the complexities of modern financial markets. This foundation not only facilitates the comprehension of stochastic volatility but also empowers the development of innovative strategies in quantitative finance.

Introduction to Itō's Lemma and Stochastic Differential Equations (SDEs)

Itō's Lemma stands as a cornerstone in the edifice of stochastic calculus, a beacon guiding the mathematical rigor of financial modeling. This powerful tool extends the classical chain rule from deterministic calculus to stochastic processes, allowing the differentiation of functions of a stochastic process. Itō's Lemma facilitates the decomposition of any smooth function of a Wiener process into its drift and diffusion components, a pivotal step in modeling the random evolution of financial variables.

The essence of Itō's Lemma lies in acknowledging the non-differentiable nature of stochastic paths, which, in turn, necessitates a unique treatment for calculus. It outlines how a function of a stochastic variable evolves over time, attributing changes not only to the direct fluctuations of the base variable but also to the inherent volatility represented by the quadratic variation of the process.

The lemma finds strategic applications in various domains of financial modeling. Its most notable application is in deriving the Black-Scholes equation for option pricing, where it elegantly captures how options' values respond to the underlying asset's stochastic movements. Furthermore, Itō's

Lemma is instrumental in formulating and solving the partial differential equations that underlie stochastic volatility models, thereby enriching our toolkit for navigating the financial markets' unpredictability.

Stochastic Differential Equations (SDEs) represent a synthesis of deterministic trends and stochastic volatility, embodying the unpredictable nature of financial markets. These equations are paramount for expressing the dynamics of asset prices and interest rates, where randomness and uncertainty are inherent.

The general form of an SDE involves a drift term, representing the expected direction of movement, and a diffusion term, capturing the random fluctuations around this trend. The Wiener process, or Brownian motion, typically models this randomness, encapsulating the erratic behavior of market variables.

Despite their daunting appearance, SDEs are tractable through numerical methods and simulations. The Euler-Maruyama method, for instance, provides a way to approximate solutions by discretizing time and simulating the path of the stochastic process. This method, alongside Monte Carlo simulations, plays a crucial role in valuing complex financial derivatives and assessing the risk inherent in volatile markets.

The interplay between Itō's Lemma and SDEs is a testament to the elegance and utility of stochastic calculus in financial modeling. Itō's Lemma offers the analytical framework needed to derive the differential equations governing the evolution of financial instruments, while SDEs provide a language to express these dynamics formally. Together, they form the backbone of quantitative finance, enabling the development of sophisticated models for option pricing, risk management, and strategic asset allocation.

Embracing Itō's Lemma and SDEs empowers financial analysts to construct and calibrate models that reflect the market's stochastic nature. From pricing exotic options to devising hedging strategies against market volatility, the combined prowess of Itō's Lemma and SDEs equips practitioners with the necessary insights to make informed decisions.

The journey into stochastic calculus opens avenues for exploring beyond traditional models. With a solid grasp of Itō's Lemma and SDEs, financial modelers are poised to harness advanced techniques such as jump diffusion models and Levy processes, further enriching the landscape of quantitative finance.

The Role of Wiener Processes in Modeling Financial Markets

In stochastic calculus and financial modeling lies the Wiener process, also known as Brownian motion, named after the botanist Robert Brown and mathematically formalized by Norbert Wiener. This mathematical construct is crucial for modeling the random motion observed in financial markets, embodying the erratic behavior of asset prices over time.

A Wiener process is characterized by its continuous, nowhere differentiable paths, which represent the incessant fluctuations in market prices. Its properties include stationary independent increments, normal distribution of increments, and continuous paths, making it a probabilistic model that captures the essence of unpredictability in financial markets.

Mathematically, a Wiener process $W(t)$ is defined by the conditions: $W(0) = 0$, $W(t) - W(s) \sim N(0, t-s)$ for $0 \leq s < t$, and the increments $W(t) - W(s)$ are independent for non-overlapping intervals. This formulation encapsulates the unpredictable nature of asset pricing, where prices can swing wildly without a discernible pattern.

The ubiquity of the Wiener process in financial modeling can largely be attributed to its foundational role in the Black-Scholes model and other stochastic differential equations (SDEs) that describe the dynamics of financial markets. Its simplicity and stochastic nature make it an ideal building block for more complex models.

In practical terms, the Wiener process is instrumental in simulating the path of asset prices under random conditions. This facilitates the pricing of derivatives, risk management, and strategic investment planning by allowing financial analysts to forecast a range of possible outcomes and devise strategies accordingly.

The Wiener process serves as the backbone for Itō's Lemma and the subsequent development of stochastic calculus. It provides a stochastic element to differential equations, enabling the modeling of financial variables as continuous but erratic processes that evolve over time.

The application of the Wiener process in option pricing is a testament to its significance in financial mathematics. By modeling the underlying asset's price movements as a Wiener process, the Black-Scholes model offers a revolutionary framework for option pricing, which has been a cornerstone in financial theory and practice.

The Wiener process introduces the concept of volatility as a key determinant of an asset's price movement. This has profound implications for understanding and managing the risks associated with financial instruments, particularly options and other derivatives.

The foundational role of the Wiener process paves the way for more sophisticated models, such as the Heston model of stochastic volatility and the Cox-Ingersoll-Ross model of interest rates. These models extend the basic framework provided by the Wiener process to capture more complex aspects of financial markets.

The Wiener process's contribution to financial modeling cannot be overstated. As the cornerstone of stochastic calculus, it enables the development of models that reflect the intrinsic randomness of financial markets. Its role extends beyond theoretical formulations, impacting practical applications in option pricing, risk management, and investment strategy. Understanding the Wiener process is essential for anyone venturing into quantitative finance, as it lays the groundwork for navigating the complexities of market behavior and the development of predictive models that drive financial innovation. Through its integration into various financial theories and models, the Wiener process continues to be a fundamental tool in the quest to decode the stochastic nature of markets, providing a lens through which the financial world's volatility and unpredictability can be understood and harnessed.

CHAPTER 2: THEORETICAL FOUNDATIONS OF STOCHASTIC VOLATILITY MODELS

Conceived by Steven Heston in 1993, the model was a response to the limitations of constant volatility frameworks, most notably the Black-Scholes model. Heston introduced a revolutionary concept: volatility itself could be stochastic, exhibiting random behavior that is correlated with the asset price's movements. This idea was not just a theoretical advancement but a practical tool for traders and risk managers, reflecting the real-world behavior of markets more accurately.

The Heston model is characterized by two stochastic differential equations (SDEs). The first describes the price dynamics of the underlying asset, incorporating a stochastic volatility term. The second SDE governs the evolution of this volatility, introducing mean reversion, volatility of volatility (vo-vol), and the correlation between asset returns and volatility changes. The equations are:

1. $dS_t = \mu S_t dt + \sqrt{v_t} S_t dW_{t}^{S}$,

2. $dv_t = \kappa (\theta - v_t) dt + \sigma \sqrt{v_t} dW_{t}^{v}$,

where:

- S_t represents the asset price at time t,

- v_t denotes the variance of the asset returns,

- μ is the expected return of the asset,

- κ represents the rate of mean reversion,

- θ is the long-term variance,

- σ is the vol-of-vol, or the volatility of the variance,

- dW_{t}^{S} and dW_{t}^{v} are two Wiener processes with correlation ρ.

These equations encapsulate the essence of the Heston model, providing a framework where volatility is not a static parameter but a dynamic entity that evolves over time.

The solution to the Heston model involves complex mathematical techniques, including Fourier transforms and characteristic functions. This allows for the derivation of a closed-form solution for European option prices, a significant advantage over numerical methods which may be computationally intensive. The Heston model's ability to generate analytical solutions for option pricing under stochastic volatility is one of its most compelling features, enabling traders to compute prices and Greeks efficiently.

The practical application of the Heston model in options pricing is vast. It provides a more nuanced view of the Greeks, reflecting the impact of stochastic volatility. Furthermore, the model's parameters can be calibrated to market data, allowing practitioners to capture the volatility surface's shape more accurately than constant volatility models. This calibration process, while , is pivotal for deploying the Heston model in real-world trading and risk management strategies.

In this analysis of the Heston model, we have traversed its theoretical underpinnings, mathematical structure, and practical applications. The model stands as a testament to the evolving understanding of market dynamics, offering a robust tool for dissecting the complexities of stochastic volatility. As we progress, this foundation will serve as a springboard into deeper explorations of volatility modeling and its implications for trading strategies.

The Model's Assumptions and Formulation

The Heston model is constructed on a foundation of carefully articulated assumptions, each playing a pivotal role in modeling stochastic volatility. These assumptions include:

1. Stochastic Volatility: The model posits that volatility is not constant but follows a stochastic process, marked by random

fluctuations over time. This assumption is a departure from simpler models where volatility is a fixed parameter, reflecting a more realistic portrayal of market conditions.

2. Mean Reversion: A key feature of the Heston model is the concept of mean reversion in volatility. The model assumes that volatility tends to drift back towards a long-term average level, θ, over time. This mean-reverting behavior is governed by the rate of reversion, κ, which indicates how quickly volatility reverts to its mean.

3. Volatility of Volatility (Vo-Vol): The Heston model introduces the idea that the volatility of the asset's returns itself has volatility, denoted by σ. This parameter reflects the uncertainty or risk associated with the volatility process, capturing the idea that volatility can exhibit significant swings.

4. Correlation between Asset Returns and Volatility: The model incorporates a correlation parameter, ρ, between the asset price's returns and the volatility process. This correlation can be positive or negative, representing the tendency of volatility to increase as the asset price decreases, and vice versa. This nuanced view of correlation adds depth to the model, accounting for the leverage effect observed in financial markets.

At its mathematical core, the Heston model is elegantly formulated through a set of stochastic differential equations that describe the dynamics of the asset price and its volatility. The model's SDEs are expressed as:

1. Asset Price Dynamics: $dS_t = \mu S_t dt + \sqrt{v_t} S_t$

$dW_{t}^{S}\)$,

2. Volatility Dynamics: $\(dv_t = \kappa (\theta - v_t) dt + \sigma \sqrt{v_t} dW_{t}^{v}\)$,

where $\(S_t\)$ and $\(v_t\)$ represent the asset price and variance at time $\(t\)$, respectively, with $\(\mu\)$ as the expected return on the asset. The terms $\(dW_{t}^{S}\)$ and $\(dW_{t}^{v}\)$ denote two Wiener processes for the asset price and volatility, reflecting their stochastic nature. The correlation between these processes is captured by $\(\rho\)$, a critical component of the model that influences the pricing of options and derivatives.

The formulation of the Heston model encapsulates a dynamic and interconnected view of markets, where the movements of asset prices and their volatility are intricately linked. This mathematical framework allows for the detailed analysis and pricing of financial instruments, accommodating the complex behaviors observed in real-world markets.

In applying the Heston model, several practical considerations emerge. The calibration of model parameters to match market data is a non-trivial challenge, requiring sophisticated optimization techniques. This process is essential for the model to accurately reflect the observed market conditions and for effective application in trading and risk management strategies.

Moreover, the computational complexity of solving the Heston model necessitates the use of numerical methods, particularly for options pricing outside of European calls and puts. These methods, while powerful, demand significant computational resources and expertise in financial engineering.

Through understanding the assumptions and formulation of the Heston model, financial practitioners and scholars can appreciate the depth and versatility of this framework. It offers a robust tool for navigating the landscapes of modern financial markets, providing insights into the behavior of asset prices under stochastic volatility. As we continue to explore the applications and implications of the Heston model, its foundational principles will guide our journey into advanced financial modeling and strategic decision-making.

Solving the Heston Model SDE

The Heston model, with its stochastic volatility and mean-reverting features, presents a complex set of equations that do not lend themselves to straightforward analytical solutions, except in some specific cases. As such, numerical methods become indispensable tools for solving the model's SDEs. The primary methods employed include:

1. Finite Difference Methods (FDM): These are grid-based numerical methods that discretize the space of possible asset prices and volatilities. By approximating the derivatives in the Heston SDEs using differences, FDM transforms the problem into a solvable system of linear equations. This method is particularly useful for calculating the price of European options under the Heston framework.

2. Monte Carlo Simulation: This method involves simulating a large number of paths for the underlying asset's price and its volatility by drawing random samples from the distributions defined by the Heston model's SDEs. Monte Carlo simulations

can accommodate the model's stochastic nature and are highly flexible, applicable to a wide range of financial instruments beyond European options, including exotic options and derivatives with path-dependent features.

3. Fourier Transform Methods: Leveraging the properties of the Fourier transform, this approach offers a semi-analytical solution to the pricing problem under the Heston model. By transforming the pricing problem into the frequency domain, complex integrals can be evaluated more conveniently. The characteristic function of the Heston model, which can be derived analytically, plays a key role in this method.

Solving the Heston model's SDE involves dealing with two intertwined stochastic processes: one for the asset price S_t and another for the variance v_t. The challenge arises from their dependence, influenced by the correlation parameter ρ, and the non-linear nature of the variance process.

The Euler-Maruyama method provides a basic yet powerful scheme for discretizing and simulating these stochastic processes. For the asset price S_t, the change over a small timestep Δt can be approximated as:

$$\Delta S_t = \mu S_t \Delta t + \sqrt{v_t} S_t \Delta W_{t}^{S}$$

Similarly, the variance v_t can be updated using:

$$\Delta v_t = \kappa (\theta - v_t) \Delta t + \sigma \sqrt{v_t} \Delta W_{t}^{v}$$

where ΔW_{t}^{S} and ΔW_{t}^{v} are increments of the Wiener processes, correlated by ρ.

The practical application of these numerical methods to solve the Heston SDE is rich with challenges. Calibration of the model to market data is a critical step, requiring optimization techniques to find the best-fitting parameters ($\kappa, \theta, \sigma, \rho$). The accuracy of solutions depends heavily on the chosen numerical method, the discretization granularity, and the computational resources available.

Moreover, the complexity of these methods and the computational cost can be significant, particularly for high-dimensional problems or instruments requiring a large number of price path simulations. Efficient implementation and the use of computational frameworks optimized for numerical analysis are therefore crucial.

Solving the Heston model SDE is a journey through complex mathematical landscapes, demanding a blend of theoretical knowledge, computational skills, and practical experience. The choice among finite difference methods, Monte Carlo simulation, and Fourier transform techniques depends on the specific financial instrument being priced, the available computational resources, and the desired accuracy of the solution. This exploration not only illuminates the versatility and power of the Heston model but also showcases the depth of quantitative finance as a discipline that intersects mathematics, finance, and computer science.

Application of the Heston Model in Option Pricing

The genesis of the Heston model's application in option pricing lies in its ability to model volatility as a stochastic process, which is a significant departure from the constant volatility assumption in the Black-Scholes model. The crux of the Heston model's theoretical appeal is its formulation of volatility as mean-reverting and subject to random fluctuations, encapsulated in a set of coupled stochastic differential equations. This formulation imbues the model with the flexibility to capture the volatility smile—a phenomenon that the Black-Scholes model, with its constant volatility premise, fails to explain.

The Heston model posits that the price of an option can be determined by solving a partial differential equation (PDE) that incorporates both the stochastic asset price and its variance. This dual stochastic nature facilitates a more nuanced capture of market conditions, enabling the pricing of options with a precision that mirrors the complexities of real-world markets.

The application of the Heston model in practical option pricing scenarios is an process that hinges on the calibration of the model to observed market prices of derivatives. This calibration process involves optimizing the model parameters —mean reversion level, mean reversion rate, volatility of volatility, long-term variance, and the correlation between the asset returns and variance process—to align the model's theoretical prices with market prices.

Numerical methods, chiefly the Fourier transform approach, have emerged as potent tools in solving the Heston model for option pricing. By applying the Fourier transform, the complex problem of evaluating the option prices under the

Heston model is transmuted into a more tractable form. The characteristic function of the Heston model, which can be derived analytically, plays a pivotal role in this method, significantly simplifying the computation of option prices.

The application of the Heston model transcends theoretical interest and extends into the practical realms of trading and risk management. Traders leverage the model to gain insights into the fair value of options in environments characterized by volatile markets. The model's parameters, gleaned from market data, facilitate the crafting of strategies that are responsive to the stochastic nature of volatility, offering a hedge against adverse movements.

Risk managers, on the other hand, utilize the Heston model to assess the risk profile of options portfolios. The model's stochastic volatility framework enables the evaluation of portfolio sensitivities (Greeks) under dynamic market conditions, enhancing the robustness of risk management practices.

The application of the Heston model in option pricing represents a paradigm shift in the valuation of financial derivatives. Through its sophisticated portrayal of volatility as a stochastic process, the Heston model offers a more accurate and dynamic framework for option pricing, invaluable for traders and risk managers alike. As we delve deeper into this model's application, its integration into quantitative finance's lexicon becomes undeniable, reflecting the dance between theory and practice that characterizes modern financial markets.

SABR and Beyond: Expanding the Horizon of Stochastic Volatility Models

The SABR model stands as a beacon of progress in the stochastic volatility modeling landscape. Developed to address the limitations of earlier models and to provide a more comprehensive framework for capturing the dynamics of financial market volatilities, the SABR model introduces a stochastic process for both the volatility and the asset price. The model is characterized by four parameters: alpha (volatility of volatility), beta (elasticity coefficient), rho (correlation between asset price and volatility), and nu (rate of mean reversion).

One of the model's most innovative aspects is its flexibility in adapting to different market conditions, including capturing the skew and smile effects observed in implied volatility surfaces. Unlike its precursors, the SABR model offers an analytically tractable approximation formula for European option pricing, making it both powerful and practical for traders and quants.

The practical implementation of the SABR model involves calibrating its parameters to fit market data, a complex task that requires sophisticated numerical techniques. The model's ability to generate implied volatility surfaces that align with observed market data underpins its utility in derivatives pricing and risk management. Furthermore, the SABR model serves as a critical tool in managing portfolios of interest rate derivatives, where modeling the evolution of volatility is crucial for accurate pricing and hedging.

The SABR model's adaptability to various asset classes and its capacity to model the volatility smile accurately make it a valuable asset in the financial modeling toolkit. Its analytic approximation formula for implied volatility facilitates the rapid assessment of options and other financial instruments, underscoring the model's practical significance.

The exploration of volatility modeling does not conclude with the SABR model. The relentless pursuit of more accurate, efficient, and comprehensive models has led to the development of extensions and entirely new frameworks. These advancements aim to address the limitations of the SABR model, such as its reliance on normal or log-normal distributions and the challenges associated with calibrating its parameters in highly volatile markets.

Emerging trends in volatility modeling include the incorporation of machine learning techniques to predict volatility patterns and the development of models that can better accommodate extreme market conditions. Furthermore, the integration of big data analytics offers the potential to harness vast datasets for improved model accuracy and insight into market dynamics.

The journey from the SABR model to the burgeoning frontier of volatility modeling encapsulates the ongoing evolution of quantitative finance. As we push beyond the confines of existing models, the quest for more sophisticated, accurate, and adaptable frameworks continues. The exploration of new methodologies and technologies heralds an exciting future for stochastic volatility modeling, promising to enhance our understanding of market complexities and improve our ability to navigate the financial landscape with precision and insight.

The SABR Model: Assumptions and Key Features

The SABR model is built on a set of precise mathematical

assumptions that enable it to capture the complex behavior of financial markets with greater fidelity. Firstly, the model assumes that the asset price and its volatility follow stochastic processes, which are correlated with each other. This correlation is pivotal in modeling the co-movement of prices and volatilities, a phenomenon often observed in real-world markets.

1. Stochastic Volatility: The volatility of the asset is not constant but follows a stochastic process, specifically a mean-reverting process. This aligns with the observed market behavior where volatility tends to fluctuate around a long-term average but can exhibit significant short-term deviations.

2. Beta Parameter: The beta parameter in the SABR model governs the elasticity of the volatility with respect to changes in the underlying asset price. This parameter can vary between 0 and 1, where a beta of 1 indicates a log-normal process (similar to Black-Scholes), and a beta of 0 suggests a normal process for the underlying asset price.

3. Correlation (Rho): The model incorporates a correlation parameter (rho) that captures the relationship between the asset price and its volatility. A negative rho indicates that the asset price and volatility move in opposite directions, a common observation in equity markets where volatility tends to increase as prices fall.

4. Volatility of Volatility (Alpha and Nu): The parameters alpha and nu represent the volatility of volatility and the rate of mean reversion, respectively. These parameters are crucial for modeling the dynamic nature of volatility and its reaction to market movements.

The SABR model introduces several key features that significantly enhance its utility in financial modeling:

1. Flexibility in Modeling Implied Volatility: The model's formula for implied volatility can adapt to various market conditions, effectively capturing the volatility smile—a curve depicting the implied volatility across different strike prices.

2. Analytical Approximation Formula: One of the SABR model's most practical contributions is its analytical approximation formula for European option pricing. This formula enables practitioners to quickly estimate option prices without resorting to computationally intensive numerical methods.

3. Application Across Asset Classes: While initially developed for interest rate markets, the SABR model's flexibility and robustness have facilitated its application across a broad spectrum of asset classes, including equities, commodities, and foreign exchange.

4. Enhanced Calibration Techniques: The calibration of the SABR model to market data is a critical step in its application. Advances in optimization algorithms and computing power have improved the efficiency and accuracy of model calibration, enabling more precise representation of market conditions.

The SABR model embodies a significant advance in stochastic volatility modeling, characterized by its sophisticated treatment of volatility and its correlation with asset prices. The assumptions underlying the model provide a robust framework for capturing market dynamics, while its key features offer practical tools for traders and risk managers. As we continue to explore the implications and applications of the SABR model, its contributions to the field of quantitative finance remain indispensable, offering insights and methodologies that drive innovation and understanding in a complex financial world.

Extension of SABR: Volatility Smile Fitting and Calibration

The volatility smile is a phenomenon in the options market where implied volatility forms a U-shaped curve across different strike prices, diverging from the constant volatility assumption of the Black-Scholes model. This pattern indicates that the market's perception of risk (and hence the price of options) varies with the strike price, challenging traditional models to accommodate such variations. The SABR model's extension towards fitting the volatility smile is a direct response to this challenge, offering a more nuanced view of market dynamics.

The process of fitting the volatility smile within the SABR framework involves a few key steps, each contributing to the model's ability to capture market realities:

1. Parameter Estimation: The first step involves estimating the parameters of the SABR model (alpha, beta, rho, and nu) that best fit the observed market prices of options across different strikes. This is typically achieved through optimization techniques that minimize the discrepancy between the model's predicted prices and the market prices.

2. Smile Dynamics: The SABR model accounts for the

dynamics of the volatility smile by allowing the shape of the smile to change with the underlying asset's price level and time to maturity. This dynamic adjustment is crucial for accurately pricing options for different strike prices and maturities.

3. Analytical Approximations: For practical purposes, the SABR model employs analytical approximations to express the implied volatility in terms of the model parameters. These approximations facilitate quick calculations and are particularly useful for real-time pricing and risk management.

4. Calibration: The calibration process involves fine-tuning the model parameters so that the SABR model's implied volatility curve fits the observed market volatility smile as closely as possible. Advanced calibration techniques often employ numerical optimization methods, exploiting the computational efficiency of the analytical approximations.

The calibration of the SABR model to the volatility smile is computationally intensive, presenting several challenges:

1. Numerical Stability: The optimization process must ensure numerical stability, particularly for options with long maturities where the smile effect is more pronounced.

2. Market Data Quality: The accuracy of calibration heavily depends on the quality and granularity of market data. Incomplete or noisy data can lead to suboptimal parameter estimates.

3. Computational Efficiency: Given the real-time needs of trading and risk management, the calibration process must

be computationally efficient. This often requires innovative numerical methods and high-performance computing resources.

The extension of the SABR model to include volatility smile fitting and calibration is a testament to the model's adaptability and its enduring relevance in financial modeling. By embracing the complexities of the volatility smile, the SABR model offers a more realistic and dynamic framework for understanding and predicting market behaviors. The ongoing advancements in computational techniques and the increasing availability of high-quality market data further enhance the model's application, ensuring its place at the forefront of quantitative finance. This detailed exploration not only underscores the technical achievements of the SABR model but also highlights the continuous effort to bridge theoretical finance and practical market realities.

Comparison of SABR with Other Stochastic Volatility Models

The Generalized Autoregressive Conditional Heteroskedasticity (GARCH) model stands in contrast to the SABR model primarily in its treatment of volatility. While the SABR model is a forward-looking model that prices derivatives by forecasting future volatility based on a stochastic process, GARCH is inherently retrospective, relying on historical price data to predict future volatility.

1. Volatility Clustering: GARCH models excel in capturing volatility clustering—a phenomenon where high-volatility events tend to cluster together in time. This characteristic makes GARCH particularly useful for risk management and analyzing securities that exhibit strong mean-reversion in volatility.

2. Predictive Nature: Unlike the SABR model, which uses a stochastic differential equation to define volatility as a forward-facing random process, GARCH predicts future volatility as a function of past squared returns and past variances. This backward-looking approach limits its use in pricing derivatives, where a predictive model of future volatility is necessary.

3. Flexibility: The SABR model, with its parameters alpha, beta, rho, and nu, offers direct control over the shape of the volatility smile, making it adaptable to a wide range of market conditions. GARCH models, while versatile in their specification, do not directly address the volatility smile, focusing instead on the time series properties of volatility.

The CGMY model, named after its creators Carr, Geman, Madan, and Yor, is a Lévy process-based model that aims to capture the jumps and heavy tails observed in asset returns, which are not accommodated by the diffusive processes of the SABR model.

1. Handling Market Jumps: One of the critical advantages of the CGMY model over SABR is its ability to accurately model sudden jumps in asset prices— a key feature during market crises or significant news events. The SABR model, being a continuous process, smoothens over such jumps, making CGMY more appropriate for assets known for their jump volatility.

2. Heavy Tails: Financial return distributions often exhibit 'fat tails,' indicating a higher probability of extreme outcomes than predicted by normal distribution. The CGMY model naturally incorporates this feature through its Lévy process

framework, offering a better fit for the empirical return distributions than the Gaussian-based SABR model.

3. Calibration Complexity: While CGMY offers nuanced insights into asset price distributions, it comes at the cost of increased complexity in calibration. The SABR model, with its analytical approximations for implied volatility, provides a more straightforward and computationally efficient approach for fitting the volatility smile.

Each stochastic volatility model, be it SABR, GARCH, or CGMY, brings a unique lens through which to view and interpret market volatility. The SABR model's strength lies in its flexibility and the direct engagement with the volatility smile, making it indispensable for derivative pricing under various market conditions. GARCH models offer invaluable insights into the temporal dynamics of volatility, suited for risk management and analyzing assets with pronounced volatility clustering. Meanwhile, the CGMY model's capacity to handle jumps and heavy tails in asset returns renders it essential for markets characterized by abrupt movements and fat-tailed distributions.

The choice between these models hinges on the specific requirements of the task at hand, whether it be derivative pricing, risk analysis, or capturing the peculiarities of asset return distributions. Through this comparative exploration, it becomes evident that a holistic understanding of market volatility necessitates an arsenal of models, each contributing its perspective to the multifaceted phenomenon of financial market dynamics.

Calibrating Stochastic Volatility Models

The primary objective of calibrating stochastic volatility models is to ensure that the model can replicate the market's implied volatility surface as closely as possible. The implied volatility surface is a three-dimensional plot showing the market implied volatility for options across various strike prices and maturities. An accurately calibrated model allows for the pricing of derivative products and risk management activities to be conducted with confidence, reflecting current market conditions.

1. Complexity of Models: Stochastic volatility models are inherently complex, involving non-linear differential equations. The calibration process, therefore, requires sophisticated numerical methods to solve these equations and optimize the model parameters.

2. Overfitting: A common challenge in the calibration process is overfitting, where the model parameters are too finely tuned to match historical data. This can result in a model that performs well on past data but poorly predicts future market conditions.

3. Computational Intensity: The calibration process can be computationally intensive, especially for complex models like the Heston model or the SABR model. This computational demand necessitates efficient algorithms and substantial computational resources.

Maximum Likelihood Estimation is a statistical method used to estimate the model parameters that maximize the likelihood function. In the context of stochastic volatility models, the likelihood function measures how probable the observed market prices are, given the model parameters. MLE is particularly useful for models where the underlying asset's price follows a continuous process.

The Least Squares method minimizes the sum of the squares of the differences between the observed market prices and the prices predicted by the model. This method is widely used in calibrating models that aim to fit the implied volatility surface, as it effectively balances the model's performance across different strike prices and maturities.

The Heston model is a widely used stochastic volatility model that requires calibration to market data for practical application. The calibration process typically involves the use of a numerical optimization technique, such as the Levenberg-Marquardt algorithm, to find the set of parameters that minimizes the difference between the model's implied volatility surface and the market observed surface.

This optimization is conducted over the parameters of the Heston model, including the long-term volatility level, the mean reversion rate, the volatility of volatility, the correlation between the underlying asset returns and the volatility, and the initial volatility level. The challenge lies in the non-linear nature of the equations involved and the sensitivity of the model's output to changes in these parameters.

The calibration of stochastic volatility models is a critical step in the application of these models to real-world financial problems. It requires a careful balance between model complexity, computational efficiency, and the avoidance of overfitting. The techniques of Maximum Likelihood Estimation and Least Squares provide robust frameworks for this calibration process, but they demand a deep understanding of the models and the numerical methods involved. Successfully calibrated models are invaluable tools in the pricing and risk management of derivative securities, offering insights into the underlying dynamics of market volatility.

Objective and Challenges of Model Calibration

The cornerstone objective of model calibration in financial engineering is to fine-tune the parameters of a stochastic volatility model such that it aligns with market data, particularly the implied volatility observed in the prices of financial derivatives. This alignment is not merely a mathematical exercise but a pragmatic approach to ensuring that the model can serve as a reliable tool for evaluating, pricing, and managing financial instruments under the current market conditions. By achieving an accurate calibration, the model's predictive capabilities are substantially enhanced, facilitating more informed decision-making in trading strategies, risk management, and financial planning.

Calibrating stochastic volatility models is fraught with challenges, each presenting a unique set of obstacles to achieving a model that is both accurate and practical.

1. Model Complexity vs. Market Simplicity: One of the principal challenges lies in the inherent complexity of stochastic volatility models. These models are constructed on sophisticated mathematical and statistical foundations, aiming to capture the stochastic nature of volatility. However, the real market data, which these models strive to replicate, often exhibits behaviors that can be at odds with the assumptions underpining the models. Bridging this gap between model complexity and market simplicity remains a

daunting task.

2. Dimensionality and Computational Constraints: As models become more refined in their attempt to capture market behaviors, the dimensionality of the calibration problem increases. This escalation not only amplifies the computational load but also introduces greater potential for the curse of dimensionality to obfuscate the calibration process. Efficient algorithms and high-performance computing resources become indispensable, yet they also impose financial and operational constraints on the calibration process.

3. Temporal Stability and Re-calibration: Financial markets are dynamic, with their volatility surface shifting in response to new information and market sentiments. This dynamism challenges the temporal stability of model calibrations. A model accurately calibrated today may not hold its precision tomorrow, necessitating frequent re-calibrations. This continuous adjustment poses both a practical challenge in terms of resources and a methodological challenge in ensuring consistency and reliability over time.

4. Avoiding Overfitting: In the quest for accuracy, there is a temptation to overfit the model to historical data, making it exceptionally good at replicating past market conditions but poor at forecasting future behaviors. Overfitting not only undermines the model's predictive power but also its utility in risk management and strategic decision-making. Striking a balance between fit and forecastability is a delicate endeavor, requiring rigorous validation techniques and a judicious approach to model complexity.

5. Market Anomalies and Structural Breaks: Financial

markets are susceptible to anomalies and structural breaks, events that can dramatically alter the volatility landscape. These occurrences present significant challenges for model calibration, as they may render previous calibrations obsolete and demand a reevaluation of model assumptions and parameters. Adapting models to account for these market phenomena without compromising their integrity is a sophisticated challenge that calibration practitioners regularly face.

The calibration of stochastic volatility models is an endeavor of paramount importance in quantitative finance, lying at the intersection of theory and practice. It requires a deep understanding of both the models in question and the market phenomena they aim to replicate. Despite the formidable challenges outlined, successful calibration unlocks the potential of these models to serve as powerful tools in the financial industry, offering insights into the complex dynamics of market volatility and enhancing the robustness of financial decision-making processes.

Techniques for Parameter Estimation: Maximum Likelihood Estimation (MLE) and Least Squares

Maximum Likelihood Estimation stands as a cornerstone statistical method for parameter estimation, renowned for its applicability across a wide range of models, including those stochastic volatility analysis. The essence of MLE lies in its objective: to find the set of parameters that make the observed market data most probable under the assumed model framework.

MLE seeks to maximize the likelihood function, which represents the probability of observing the current market data given specific model parameters. This process involves a detailed examination of the parameter space, identifying the point where the likelihood peaks, signaling the optimal parameter values.

For stochastic volatility models, MLE can be particularly insightful. By aligning the model's predictions with observed option prices or returns, MLE helps quantify how well the model captures the underlying market dynamics, offering a pathway to refine the model's accuracy.

Despite its prowess, MLE is not without its challenges. The complexity of the likelihood function, especially in high-dimensional models typical in finance, can lead to computational difficulties. Moreover, the presence of local maxima may complicate the search for the global maximum, necessitating sophisticated optimization algorithms.

Parallel to MLE, the Least Squares method offers another avenue for parameter estimation, particularly revered for its simplicity and effectiveness in models where the relationship between model parameters and market observations is linear or can be linearized.

The Least Squares method minimizes the sum of the squared differences between the observed market values and the values predicted by the model, given a set of parameters. This minimization leads to a set of optimal parameters that best fit the observed data.

In the context of stochastic volatility, the Least Squares approach is adept at handling scenarios where the relationship between some aspects of market data (like the squares of asset returns) and model parameters is approximately linear. It's particularly useful in the initial stages of model calibration, providing a quick, albeit approximate, parameter estimation.

While advantageous for its computational simplicity, the Least Squares method may not always reach the level of precision required for complex models or in the presence of non-linear relationships. Its reliance on a "close-enough" linear approximation may lead to biases in parameter estimation, especially in models sensitive to parameter nuances.

The journey of model calibration in quantitative finance is often a tale of balancing precision with practicality. In this narrative, MLE and the Least Squares method play complementary roles. MLE, with its probabilistic foundations, offers a depth of analysis conducive to fine-tuning models to market dynamics. Simultaneously, the Least Squares method provides a broad-brush tool, efficient for initial calibrations and models with simpler dynamics.

The art of model calibration involves leveraging these techniques judiciously, often starting with the Least Squares method for a baseline calibration before delving into the more computationally intensive but precise MLE for final adjustments. This phased approach facilitates a calibration process that is both practical and robust, capable of adapting stochastic volatility models to the multifarious nature of financial markets.

The calibration of stochastic volatility models is a nuanced process, requiring a blend of statistical rigor and computational acumen. Maximum Likelihood Estimation and the Least Squares method stand out as fundamental techniques in this process, each with its strengths and limitations. Understanding and applying these methods in concert can significantly enhance the fidelity of model calibrations, bridging the gap between theoretical constructs and the complex realities of financial markets.

Calibration of the Heston Model Using Market Data

Before we embark on the calibration process, it's pertinent to revisit the Heston model's fundamental structure. The model is characterized by two stochastic differential equations (SDEs): one governing the asset price dynamics and another for the volatility process. The essence of the Heston model lies in its ability to model volatility as a mean-reverting square root process, capturing the observed volatility smile in option markets.

The calibration process begins with the preparation of market data, typically option prices across different strikes and maturities. The quality and selection of data are paramount; it must be relevant, accurate, and comprehensive, encompassing a wide range of market conditions. This data preparation stage involves cleaning, normalization, and, crucially, the computation of implied volatilities from market option prices, which serve as the primary inputs for calibration.

The cornerstone of the calibration process is the definition of an objective function that quantifies the difference between market observed quantities (implied volatilities) and those produced by the model under certain parameters. The sum of squared errors (SSE) between the market and model implied volatilities is a commonly used objective function.

The calibration involves an optimization routine that seeks to minimize the objective function. This process requires a careful selection of optimization algorithms capable of navigating the complex, multi-dimensional parameter space of the Heston model. Gradient-based methods, global optimization techniques, or heuristic algorithms like genetic algorithms are commonly employed.

To ensure the feasibility and stability of the calibrated model, constraints on parameter values are often imposed based on empirical observations and theoretical bounds. Furthermore, regularization techniques may be applied to avoid overfitting, especially when the market data is noisy or sparse.

Calibrating the Heston model is not without its challenges. The non-linear nature of the model, coupled with the potential for multiple local minima in the optimization landscape, can complicate the calibration process. Additionally, market data imperfections, such as bid-ask spreads and temporal gaps in data availability, introduce further complexity.

Post-calibration, it's crucial to test the model against out-of-sample data to assess its predictive power and robustness. This step ensures that the calibrated model is not merely a reflection of the specific dataset used for calibration but a reliable tool for broader market analysis.

Conducting sensitivity analysis on the calibrated parameters can provide insights into how changes in market conditions might affect the model's outputs. This analysis is essential for understanding the model's limitations and areas of potential improvement.

Calibration is not a one-time exercise but an iterative process. As new market data becomes available or as market conditions evolve, the model may require re-calibration to maintain its relevance and accuracy.

The calibration of the Heston model using market data is a meticulous process that blends statistical techniques with practical market insights. It's a crucial step in tailoring the model to capture the complexities of financial markets accurately. Through careful preparation of market data, methodical optimization, and rigorous post-calibration analysis, the calibrated Heston model emerges as a powerful tool for option pricing, risk management, and strategic financial analysis.

CHAPTER 3: PRACTICAL IMPLICATIONS AND LIMITATIONS

To understand the application of stochastic volatility models in trading, it's crucial to grasp the concept of volatility itself —a measure of the dispersion of returns for a given security or market index. Traditional models often assumed constant volatility, an oversimplification that could lead to strategies ill-suited for real-world markets. Stochastic volatility models, however, recognize volatility as a dynamic entity, influenced by a myriad of factors and capable of fluctuating independently of the asset price.

The Heston model, for instance, is a pioneering stochastic volatility model that allows volatility to follow its own stochastic process, thereby introducing a more realistic framework for option pricing and trading strategies. By modeling two random processes—one for the asset price and one for its volatility—traders can gain insights into the potential range of future price movements, an invaluable asset in forming trading decisions.

Hedging, the practice of taking an offsetting position to

mitigate risk, finds a robust ally in stochastic volatility models. These models enable the calculation of "Greeks" (delta, gamma, vega, theta, and rho), which measure the sensitivity of the option's price to various factors. Understanding these sensitivities allows traders to construct hedging strategies that can adapt to changes in the underlying asset's price, interest rates, and, crucially, its volatility.

Consider a trader holding a portfolio of options who uses the Heston model to hedge against market movements. By observing the vega, which measures sensitivity to volatility, the trader can adjust their portfolio to become vega-neutral, thus insulating it from small shifts in volatility. Such precision in hedging was less attainable with models that treated volatility as a static parameter.

To operationalize these concepts, traders employ scenario analysis and stress testing, using stochastic volatility models to simulate a wide range of market conditions. For example, a trader might use the Heston model to generate potential future paths for both the asset price and its volatility under scenarios of market turmoil, such as a financial crisis or geopolitical conflict. By analyzing these paths, traders can identify strategies that would perform well across diverse conditions, optimizing their trading and hedging positions accordingly.

Let's consider a practical example involving an equity option. Assume a trader wants to hedge an option portfolio against movements in the underlying stock, S, with current volatility σ. Using the Heston model, the trader simulates several possible future paths for S and σ, calculating the option portfolio's delta and vega at each step. To hedge against price movements, the trader takes positions in the stock to offset delta. Simultaneously, to hedge against volatility risk, the trader takes positions in options with differing sensitivities to volatility (vega hedging), such as options on the same stock with different strikes or maturities.

This dual strategy of delta and vega hedging allows the trader to minimize the portfolio's sensitivity to both price and volatility changes. It exemplifies the nuanced approach required when trading and hedging with stochastic volatility models, moving beyond simplistic strategies that might only consider price movements.

Trading and hedging in the face of stochastic volatility embody the synthesis of sophisticated mathematical models with strategic market actions. The adaptation of stochastic volatility models, such as the Heston and SABR models, has endowed traders and risk managers with a more nuanced understanding of market dynamics, enabling strategies that are both resilient and adaptable. As we continue to venture deeper into the complexities of financial markets, the evolution of these models and their applications in trading and hedging strategies remains a critical area of exploration for practitioners and academics alike.

How Traders Use Stochastic Volatility Models for Hedging Options

Stochastic volatility models, such as the Heston and SABR models, offer a realistic representation of how volatility behaves—unpredictable, random, and crucially, independent of the asset's price movement. This attribute makes them indispensable in options trading and hedging strategies. Unlike traditional models where volatility is a constant, stochastic volatility models account for the volatility's erratic nature, providing a dynamic framework that aligns more closely with real-world market conditions.

hedging with options under stochastic volatility models lies the understanding of 'Vega'—the option's price sensitivity to changes in volatility. A positive vega indicates an option's price will increase if the volatility increases, and vice versa. Traders meticulously monitor the vega of their options portfolio, adjusting their positions to manage the portfolio's overall sensitivity to volatility changes. This process, known as vega hedging, is a cornerstone of risk management in options trading.

Dynamic hedging is a strategy that involves continuously adjusting the hedge positions as market conditions change. Stochastic volatility models play a pivotal role here, particularly through the use of Greeks like delta and vega. Traders utilize these models to forecast potential shifts in the market's volatility and adjust their hedging strategies in real-time, ensuring the portfolio's exposure to market risks is minimized.

For instance, consider a scenario where a trader anticipates an increase in market volatility based on their analysis using the Heston model. To hedge against this anticipated risk, the trader might increase the portfolio's vega by purchasing options with higher vega values. Conversely, if a decrease in volatility is anticipated, the trader might reduce the portfolio's vega by selling some of these options.

The practical implementation of stochastic volatility models for hedging begins with the calibration of these models to current market conditions. Calibrating models like Heston or SABR involves fitting them to market data to ensure their parameters accurately reflect the current market environment. Once calibrated, these models can simulate various market scenarios, including extreme events or 'stress tests,' helping traders to devise hedging strategies that are robust across different market conditions.

A practical example of this application is in constructing a delta-vega neutral portfolio. By using the outputs from a stochastic volatility model, a trader can determine the appropriate mix of options and underlying assets to achieve a balance, where the portfolio's sensitivity to both price and volatility movements is minimized. This might involve a combination of buying and selling options with varying strikes and maturities, alongside positions in the underlying asset, to achieve the desired delta and vega levels.

One of the key advantages of using stochastic volatility models for hedging is their forward-looking nature. Unlike historical volatility, which looks backward, stochastic models provide a predictive view of volatility, offering insights into how volatility could evolve in the future. This predictive capability enables traders to prepare for a range of potential market conditions, making their hedging strategies more proactive and adaptive.

The nuanced application of stochastic volatility models for hedging options underscores the sophistication required in modern financial markets. By embracing the dynamic and stochastic nature of volatility, traders can craft hedging strategies that are not only reactive but also anticipatory, offering a buffer against the market's whims. As these models continue to evolve, so too will the strategies derived from them, promising a perpetually adapting landscape in the art and science of options hedging.

The Concept of "Greeks" in Managing Risks of Options Portfolios

Delta, represented as Δ, measures an option's price sensitivity to a small change in the price of the underlying asset. It is often interpreted as the "hedge ratio," indicating how many units of the underlying asset are needed to hedge the option's risk. For a call option, delta ranges between 0 and 1, while for a put option, it ranges between -1 and 0. Traders use delta to construct delta-neutral portfolios—where the net delta of all positions is zero, theoretically insulating the portfolio against small movements in the underlying asset's price.

Gamma (Γ) denotes the rate of change in an option's delta per one-unit change in the underlying asset's price. It is a measure of the curvature or the convexity of the option's value, relative to the underlying price. A high gamma indicates that the delta is highly sensitive to changes in the underlying price, providing insights into the stability of a delta-hedged portfolio. In practice, traders monitor gamma to adjust their delta hedges, especially in portfolios with options nearing expiration, where gamma tends to increase.

Theta (Θ) represents an option's sensitivity to the passage of time, often termed as "time decay." It quantifies the rate at which an option's value declines as it approaches expiration. For options traders, theta is a double-edged sword; it erodes the value of long positions day by day but benefits the seller of the options (the option writer). Portfolio managers use theta to gauge the time risk in their options portfolio, strategically selling options to harvest the premium from time decay, especially in sideways markets.

Vega measures an option's price sensitivity to a 1% change in the implied volatility of the underlying asset. Unlike the other Greeks, vega is not represented by a Greek letter. High vega values indicate that an option's price is highly susceptible to changes in volatility, making vega a critical measure for portfolios in volatile markets. Traders use vega to construct volatility-neutral portfolios, ensuring that the portfolio's value remains relatively stable despite fluctuations in market volatility.

Rho (ρ) assesses an option's sensitivity to changes in the risk-free interest rate, indicating how the value of an option might change with a 1% change in interest rates. Although often less significant than the other Greeks, in environments of shifting monetary policy or stark changes in interest rates, rho becomes an important consideration for long-term options.

Consider a portfolio manager who constructs a delta-neutral portfolio to hedge against small price movements in the underlying asset. However, as market conditions evolve, the manager frequently reassesses the portfolio's gamma to ensure that the delta hedge remains effective. Simultaneously, they might sell options with high theta to capitalize on time decay, while maintaining a vega-neutral stance to buffer against volatility risk. In a rising interest rate environment, the portfolio's rho would also be scrutinized, adjusting positions in long-term options where necessary.

The Greeks are indispensable tools in the options trader's arsenal, providing a multidimensional understanding of risk and exposure in options portfolios. By deftly managing delta, gamma, theta, vega, and rho, traders can sculpt portfolios that are resilient to the multifarious risks inherent in the options market. This elaborate dance with the Greeks embodies the nuanced equilibrium between risk and return, guiding traders through the tempestuous seas of options trading with precision and insight.

Scenario Analysis and Stress Testing Using Stochastic Models

Scenario analysis involves the examination of specific hypothetical events to assess their potential impact on investment portfolios or financial institutions. These scenarios may range from plausible market conditions, such as interest rate hikes or commodity price shocks, to extreme 'black swan' events that are unlikely but would have significant consequences if they occurred. Stochastic models facilitate this analysis by allowing for the simulation of a wide array of possible outcomes based on historical data and statistical methods.

Example: Consider a portfolio heavily invested in oil futures. Using a stochastic model like the Geometric Brownian Motion (GBM), a risk manager can simulate various scenarios, such as a sudden surge in oil prices due to geopolitical tensions or a drastic drop due to technological advancements in renewable energy. By assessing the portfolio's performance across these scenarios, the manager can gauge the potential risks and returns, guiding strategic decisions to hedge or diversify the portfolio accordingly.

Stress testing takes scenario analysis a step further by focusing on extreme conditions and assessing the resilience of financial entities against them. It involves creating highly adverse yet plausible scenarios to evaluate the threshold limits of an institution's risk exposure and capital adequacy. Stochastic volatility models, like the Heston model, are particularly suited for stress testing as they can capture the erratic movements in market volatility, which are often observed during crises.

Example: A bank might use a stochastic volatility model to simulate a severe economic downturn scenario, where GDP contracts significantly, unemployment rates soar, and market volatility spikes. The model would generate potential outcomes for the bank's asset values, loan defaults, and liquidity positions, enabling the bank to evaluate its capacity to absorb losses and meet short-term obligations without breaching regulatory capital requirements.

In practice, scenario analysis and stress testing are not isolated exercises but are integrated into a comprehensive risk management framework. They inform decision-making on various fronts, including capital allocation, risk appetite setting, and contingency planning.

1. Capital Allocation: By identifying potential risks under different scenarios, institutions can allocate capital more efficiently, ensuring sufficient buffers against losses.

2. Risk Appetite Setting: Understanding the impact of adverse conditions helps in setting thresholds for risk tolerance, guiding both strategic planning and day-to-day risk-taking activities.

3. Contingency Planning: Scenario analysis and stress testing highlight potential vulnerabilities, prompting the development of contingency plans to address these risks

proactively.

While powerful, scenario analysis and stress testing using stochastic models come with challenges. The accuracy of these models depends on the quality of the input data and the assumptions underlying the model's structure. Over-reliance on historical data may fail to capture future discontinuities, and the complexity of models can obscure their interpretability. Therefore, it's crucial to complement these techniques with qualitative assessments and expert judgment.

Scenario analysis and stress testing, underpinned by stochastic models, are indispensable in the modern financial landscape. They provide a structured way to anticipate and prepare for potential market disruptions, thereby enhancing the resilience of financial institutions. As the global economic environment grows more interconnected and volatile, these tools will continue to evolve, becoming ever more integral to financial risk management strategies.

Model Limitations and Critiques

Stochastic models are built on mathematical and statistical foundations that attempt to mirror the randomness observed in financial markets. Yet, one of the primary criticisms levied against them centers on their reliance on historical data and the assumption that past behavior can offer insights into future outcomes. This backward-looking approach can sometimes fail to account for unprecedented events or structural market changes, leading to inaccurate predictions and potential mismanagement of risk.

Example: The 2008 financial crisis serves as a poignant illustration of this limitation. Many models failed to predict the magnitude of the crisis, primarily because they could not foresee the confluence of factors that led to the market collapse. The reliance on historical market conditions meant that the models were unprepared for a scenario where housing prices fell nationwide in the United States, challenging the assumption that such an event was highly improbable based on past data.

Beyond the limitations inherent in their design, stochastic models face critiques from various quarters of the financial community. One significant area of concern is the models' complexity and the opacity that often accompanies it. For decision-makers, deciphering the outputs of complex models and understanding the assumptions and variables that drive their results can be daunting. This "black box" nature of some stochastic models can obscure the intuition behind risk assessments and investment decisions, making it challenging to fully trust or comprehend their guidance.

Example: The complexity and perceived opacity of the Gaussian copula models, which were used to price Collateralized Debt Obligations (CDOs), were highlighted as contributing factors to the 2008 crisis. The difficulty in understanding these models' inner workings and their sensitivity to underlying assumptions about correlation led to widespread mispricing of risk and contributed to the financial turmoil.

In response to these limitations and critiques, the field of stochastic modeling is continuously evolving, with researchers and practitioners striving to develop more robust, transparent, and adaptable models. This involves not only refining existing models but also incorporating new data sources, embracing advancements in computational techniques, and integrating insights from fields such as behavioral finance that challenge traditional assumptions about market efficiency and rationality.

Moreover, there is an increasing emphasis on model validation and stress testing, going beyond conventional scenarios to include extreme "tail events." These efforts aim to ensure that models can withstand rare but impactful events, providing a more comprehensive view of potential risks.

Amidst the advancements and ongoing refinements, a consensus has emerged on the importance of complementing stochastic models with human judgment. The recognition that models are tools — valuable yet imperfect — underscores the need for experienced professionals to interpret model outputs, consider qualitative factors, and apply their understanding of market nuances. This holistic approach, blending quantitative modeling with qualitative assessment, represents a maturation in the field's perspective on risk management and decision-making.

While stochastic models are indispensable in the financial sector, their limitations and the critiques they face are equally critical in pushing the boundaries of financial modeling forward. Acknowledging these challenges is not an indictment of the models but a necessary step towards their evolution. By continuously refining their approaches and appreciating the blend of art and science that financial modeling entails, professionals can leverage these tools more effectively, enhancing their capacity to navigate the complexities of the financial markets.

Identifying the Limitations of Current Stochastic Volatility Models

One notable limitation of stochastic volatility models lies in their sensitivity to initial conditions and parameter choices. The calibration of these models often requires fine-tuning, with their outputs being highly sensitive to the chosen parameters.

Example: The Heston model, known for its ability to capture the leptokurtic nature of asset returns and stochastic volatility, illustrates this challenge. The assumptions regarding the long-term average volatility, mean reversion rate, and the volatility of volatility parameter can dramatically influence the model's predictions. If these parameters are misestimated, the model may significantly misprice options or misforecast future volatility, leading to potential losses in trading strategies.

Stochastic volatility models typically assume market continuity, neglecting the impact of discrete events that can cause sudden jumps in asset prices or volatility levels. This assumption often overlooks the market's reaction to unforeseen news or events, which can lead to significant pricing and risk management errors.

Example: The Flash Crash of May 2010, where the Dow Jones Industrial Average abruptly plunged about 9% only to recover those losses within minutes, exemplifies a scenario poorly captured by continuous models. The event underscored the necessity for incorporating jump components in volatility models to account for such anomalies.

The calibration of stochastic volatility models to market data is a complex and computationally intensive process. The need to estimate multiple parameters, often under conditions of uncertainty and noise in market data, presents a significant challenge. This complexity can render the models less tractable and more time-consuming to apply in fast-paced market environments.

Example: Calibrating the SABR model involves fitting it to the implied volatility surface, a task that necessitates advanced numerical methods and optimization techniques. The computational burden associated with this process can be prohibitive, particularly when dealing with large datasets or in high-frequency trading scenarios where speed is of the essence.

Many stochastic volatility models rely heavily on historical data for calibration, assuming that past patterns of volatility will persist into the future. This reliance can be problematic during periods of structural change or when the market regime shifts in unexpected ways.

Example: The Global Financial Crisis of 2008 is a stark reminder of the pitfalls of depending on historical data. The models of the time failed to predict the surge in volatility and correlation across asset classes, as they were largely based on "peaceful" periods and did not adequately account for the possibility of systemic shocks.

In identifying the limitations of current stochastic volatility models, it becomes evident that while these models serve as powerful tools for understanding and navigating financial markets, they are not foolproof. The complexities of model calibration, the assumptions underpinning the models, and their dependence on historical data present significant challenges. Recognizing these limitations is crucial for the ongoing development and refinement of stochastic volatility models, encouraging a more nuanced approach that incorporates both quantitative analysis and qualitative judgment. As the field progresses, the quest for more adaptable, accurate, and comprehensive models continues, reflecting the ever-changing landscape of the financial markets they seek to decode.

Discussion on the Predictability of Volatility and Market Efficiency

The Efficient Market Hypothesis (EMH) posits that it is impossible to consistently achieve higher returns than average market returns on a risk-adjusted basis, given that asset prices already incorporate and reflect all relevant information. However, the observable fluctuations in market volatility contradict the EMH to some extent, indicating that markets may not always operate efficiently.

Example: The Dotcom Bubble of the late 1990s and early 2000s provides a case in point. During this period, the NASDAQ Composite index saw an unprecedented rise fueled by speculative investments in internet-based companies, followed by a dramatic collapse. The bubble's growth and burst were driven by investor irrationality rather than new, substantive information, suggesting a disconnect between market prices and underlying economic fundamentals. This phenomenon challenges the EMH, illustrating how volatility can arise from factors beyond just new information.

A key feature of financial markets is volatility clustering, where high-volatility periods tend to follow high-volatility periods, and low-volatility phases tend to follow low-volatility phases. This characteristic suggests some degree of predictability in market volatility, contrary to what one might expect in a fully efficient market.

Example: The global financial crisis of 2008 is a prime example of volatility clustering. Following the collapse of Lehman Brothers, markets around the world experienced high levels of volatility. This period was marked by a significant increase in the volatility of asset prices, which persisted as aftershocks continued to affect global markets. The ability to predict such clustered volatility can offer valuable insights for risk management and trading strategies, highlighting a deviation from the random walk theory implied by the EMH.

Stochastic volatility models, with their ability to capture the random nature of volatility, play a crucial role in understanding and predicting market movements. These models, by accounting for the stochastic nature of volatility, offer a nuanced view of market dynamics that challenges the traditional EMH perspective.

Example: The Heston model, a well-regarded stochastic volatility model, allows for the volatility of an asset to be stochastic, providing a more accurate representation of real-world market conditions. By modeling volatility as a variable that itself follows a stochastic process, the Heston model acknowledges the inherent unpredictability of markets while simultaneously allowing for certain patterns, such as volatility clustering, to be captured and potentially forecasted.

The predictability of volatility, as suggested by the presence of volatility clustering and the application of sophisticated stochastic models, has profound implications for traders, risk managers, and policymakers. It suggests that while markets may be efficient in incorporating information into prices, inefficiencies in the form of predictable volatility patterns do exist. These inefficiencies can be exploited for risk management, portfolio optimization, and strategic trading decisions.

Example: Consider a proprietary trading firm that utilizes algorithmic trading strategies based on stochastic volatility models. By identifying periods of expected high volatility, the firm can adjust its trading algorithms to either capitalize on the increased market movement or hedge against potential losses, thus navigating the market more effectively than what pure EMH would suggest is possible.

The discussion on the predictability of volatility and market efficiency unveils a landscape marked by complexity and nuanced understandings of market behavior. While the EMH provides a foundational framework for understanding market dynamics, the observable characteristics of volatility and the capabilities of stochastic volatility models reveal layers of predictability that challenge the hypothesis. Recognizing these patterns and the role of models in forecasting volatility is paramount for market participants aiming to navigate financial markets with acumen and agility.

The Impact of Market Microstructure and Liquidity on Model Performance

Market microstructure refers to the mechanisms and processes that facilitate the trading of assets within financial markets. It encompasses the organization of trading venues, the behavior of market participants, and the rules governing transactions. The structure of a market can profoundly impact information flow, price formation, and, ultimately, the volatility of asset prices.

Example: The advent of electronic trading platforms and the rise of high-frequency trading (HFT) operations have transformed market microstructure. HFT strategies, capable of executing orders in milliseconds, can cause rapid changes in liquidity and volatility. Consider the "Flash Crash" of May 6, 2010, when the Dow Jones Industrial Average plummeted nearly 1,000 points in minutes before recovering. This event underscored how changes in market microstructure, particularly the proliferation of algorithmic trading, can result in sudden volatility spikes that traditional models may struggle to predict.

Liquidity, defined as the ease with which an asset can be bought or sold without causing a significant price movement, is a cornerstone of market efficiency. High liquidity is associated with smaller price changes, while low liquidity can lead to larger, unpredictable price movements, affecting the volatility observed in the market.

Example: During periods of financial turmoil, such as the 2008 Global Financial Crisis, liquidity can evaporate rapidly, leading to increased volatility. The crisis highlighted how liquidity can swiftly decline as market participants withdraw, prompting a reevaluation of risk management strategies and the models that underpin them. Stochastic volatility models that neglect the dynamic nature of liquidity may fail to capture these critical shifts, underscoring the need for models that incorporate liquidity parameters.

The performance of stochastic volatility models in real-world trading scenarios is intricately linked to their ability to account for the complexities of market microstructure and liquidity. Traditional models often assume constant liquidity and overlook the nuances of market microstructure, potentially leading to discrepancies between predicted and observed market behaviors.

Example: The Heston model, while incorporating stochastic volatility, does not explicitly factor in variations in liquidity or changes in market microstructure. To enhance the model's applicability, extensions that account for liquidity shocks and the impact of microstructural changes have been proposed. For instance, adapting the Heston model to include a liquidity parameter that adjusts volatility based on observed liquidity levels could improve its predictive accuracy during periods of market stress.

To mitigate the discrepancies between model predictions and actual market conditions, researchers and practitioners are increasingly focusing on integrating market microstructure and liquidity considerations into stochastic volatility models. This involves developing models that are sensitive to the rapid changes in liquidity and can adapt to the evolving landscape of market microstructure.

Example: A promising approach involves coupling stochastic volatility models with machine learning techniques to dynamically adjust to changes in market conditions. By training models on high-frequency data, capturing both normal trading conditions and periods of stress, these advanced models can learn to anticipate shifts in liquidity and adjust volatility predictions accordingly. Such hybrid models represent the frontier of quantitative finance, marrying traditional modeling techniques with the power of data-driven insights.

The interplay between market microstructure, liquidity, and stochastic volatility models is a complex but crucial area of exploration for financial modeling. As markets continue to evolve, the need for models that accurately reflect these dynamics becomes increasingly paramount. By embracing the challenges posed by market microstructure and liquidity, model developers can enhance the robustness and predictive power of their models, paving the way for more resilient and effective trading strategies in the face of financial market complexities.

Future Directions in Volatility Modeling

One of the most exciting developments in volatility modeling is the integration of machine learning (ML) and artificial intelligence (AI) techniques. These technologies offer unparalleled capabilities in pattern recognition, predictive analytics, and data processing speed, presenting novel opportunities to enhance volatility models.

Example: Deep learning, a subset of ML, has shown potential in capturing the complex, nonlinear relationships inherent in financial markets. For instance, recurrent neural networks (RNNs), known for their ability to process sequential data, could be harnessed to predict volatility patterns based on historical price movements and trading volume. By training these models on vast datasets, they can uncover hidden patterns that traditional models may overlook.

The proliferation of high-frequency trading (HFT) has generated a wealth of data, offering a granular view of market dynamics. Utilizing this high-frequency data for real-time analytics represents a significant opportunity for volatility modeling. The ability to analyze data at such a fine resolution can lead to more accurate and timely assessments of market volatility.

Example: The implementation of real-time volatility models could transform risk management practices by providing up-to-the-minute insights into market conditions. For example, a model that dynamically adjusts to incoming high-frequency data could alert traders to emerging volatility spikes, allowing for rapid response to mitigate risk.

Hybrid models, which blend traditional stochastic volatility frameworks with empirical data insights, are gaining traction. These models aim to leverage the strengths of both approaches — the theoretical rigor of stochastic models and the real-world relevance of empirical data.

Example: A hybrid model might incorporate the mean-reverting nature of the Heston model while also integrating machine learning-derived indicators of market sentiment from news articles or social media. Such a model could adjust its volatility forecasts based on both quantitative market data and qualitative insights into investor behavior.

Quantum computing presents a long-term but potentially revolutionary opportunity for volatility modeling. With its superior processing power, quantum computing could perform complex calculations that are currently impractical, such as simulating entire market ecosystems to predict volatility under an array of scenarios.

Example: Quantum algorithms could be developed to solve stochastic differential equations underlying volatility models far more efficiently than classical computers. This could enable the execution of simulations that incorporate a broader range of variables, including those from macroeconomic indicators or geopolitical events, providing a more comprehensive view of factors influencing volatility.

As volatility modeling techniques become more advanced, ethical and regulatory considerations will become increasingly important. Ensuring transparency, fairness, and privacy in the use of AI and ML in finance will be paramount. Models must be designed with accountability in mind, capable of explaining decisions and predictions to satisfy regulatory requirements and maintain investor trust.

Example: Regulators might require that AI-driven volatility models undergo rigorous testing and validation to ensure they do not introduce systemic risk. Additionally, ethical guidelines could be established to govern the use of personal data in modeling market sentiment, protecting investor privacy while harnessing insights from social media and other sources.

The future of volatility modeling is rich with possibilities, as new technologies and methodologies promise to enhance our understanding and management of market volatility. From the integration of AI and ML to the potential of quantum computing, these advancements offer a glimpse into a future where volatility models are more accurate, comprehensive, and responsive to market dynamics. As we navigate this evolving landscape, the challenge will be to harness these innovations responsibly, ensuring that they contribute to a more stable and transparent financial system.

Emerging Trends and Research in Stochastic Volatility Modeling

The relentless pace of innovation in the field of quantitative finance continues to push the boundaries of what's possible with stochastic volatility modeling. As we venture deeper into a data-driven era, emerging trends and cutting-edge research are shaping the future of how we understand, model, and leverage volatility for strategic advantage. This segment delves into the forefront of stochastic volatility modeling, outlining the groundbreaking approaches that are setting the stage for the next generation of financial models.

The traditional datasets used in volatility modeling are being augmented by a surge in alternative data sources. These include satellite images, transactional data from mobile payments, and social media sentiment analysis, among others. The challenge and opportunity lie in effectively integrating this data to enhance the predictive power of volatility models.

Example: By analyzing social media sentiment in real time, a model could adjust its volatility forecasts based on the public's reaction to a corporate earnings announcement or geopolitical event. This integration of unstructured data requires sophisticated natural language processing (NLP) techniques but offers a more nuanced view of market dynamics.

Blockchain technology presents a novel foundation for developing and implementing stochastic volatility models. The immutable and transparent nature of blockchain can facilitate the creation of decentralized financial instruments, with volatility models that are auditable in real time and resistant to manipulation.

Example: A blockchain-based platform could host a decentralized volatility index, updated in real time by a network of participants rather than a central authority. This could provide a more democratic and possibly more accurate reflection of market volatility, grounded in consensus rather than singular methodology.

Computational advancements, particularly in GPU (Graphics Processing Unit) computing and parallel processing, are enabling more complex simulations and faster model calibration. These technologies allow for the exploration of models that were previously too computationally intensive to be practical.

Example: Utilizing GPU computing for Monte Carlo simulations enables the rapid evaluation of thousands of potential outcomes based on different volatility scenarios. This capability allows traders and risk managers to better assess the range of possible market movements and prepare more effectively for extreme events.

Recent research has focused on leveraging machine learning to better understand and predict volatility clustering - the phenomenon where high-volatility events tend to follow each other. By applying clustering algorithms and deep learning models to historical data, researchers aim to uncover patterns that preempt periods of high volatility.

Example: A deep learning model might be trained to recognize the precursors of volatility clustering, such as specific combinations of market conditions and investor behavior. This would enable preemptive adjustments to trading strategies, potentially mitigating risk during turbulent periods.

As AI becomes more deeply integrated into financial modeling, the emphasis on ethical AI is paramount. This involves ensuring that models do not inadvertently perpetuate biases present in historical data or violate privacy through the misuse of sensitive information.

Example: Implementing ethical AI practices could involve the use of anonymized data when training models to predict market sentiment based on investor communications. Additionally, continuous monitoring is required to identify and correct any biases that AI models might learn over time.

The landscape of stochastic volatility modeling is rapidly evolving, driven by advances in technology, computational methods, and data availability. From the integration of alternative data sources to the ethical application of AI, these emerging trends and areas of research promise to significantly enhance the accuracy, reliability, and applicability of volatility models. As we push forward, the challenge will be to adapt these innovations responsibly, ensuring they align with regulatory standards and contribute positively to market stability and investor confidence.

Considerations for Adapting Models to High-Frequency Trading Environments

The transition of stochastic volatility models into high-frequency trading (HFT) environments requires meticulous adaptation and consideration. High-frequency trading, characterized by rapid trade execution, extensive data analysis, and algorithmic strategies, demands models that are not only accurate but also exceedingly fast and responsive to market dynamics. This segment explores the multifaceted considerations necessary for refining and deploying stochastic volatility models within such fast-paced markets, aiming to highlight the challenges and innovations that accompany this adaptation.

In the domain of HFT, the ability to process data in real-time is paramount. Stochastic volatility models must be optimized to handle a deluge of data inputs without significant delays.

Example: Implementing in-memory computing techniques can drastically reduce the latency experienced during the data retrieval and computation processes, ensuring that the model's output is generated swiftly enough to inform trading decisions in near real-time.

A critical balance must be struck between the complexity of the model and the speed of execution. While more models may offer enhanced accuracy, they also tend to require more processing power and time, which can be detrimental in an HFT environment.

Example: To address this, quant developers might employ dimensionality reduction techniques on the input data or streamline the model by identifying and retaining only the most impactful variables. This way, the model remains robust but is leaner and faster, making it suitable for HFT applications.

As models are adapted for HFT, scalability becomes a concern. The model must be capable of scaling up to accommodate increased data volumes without degradation in performance.

Example: The application of parallel computing paradigms, such as utilizing GPUs for their superior processing capabilities, allows stochastic volatility models to analyze vast datasets simultaneously. This parallelism significantly enhances the model's throughput and scalability.

The microstructure of financial markets—comprising the processes, institutions, and mechanisms affecting the trading of securities—plays a crucial role in HFT. Models must be adaptable to the nuances of specific market microstructures to remain effective.

Example: By incorporating order book dynamics into the model, traders can better predict short-term volatility based on the depth of the market and the distribution of buy and sell orders. This requires a sophisticated understanding of the market microstructure and an ability to integrate these dynamics into the stochastic model.

High-frequency trading environments are particularly susceptible to market manipulations, such as quote stuffing or layering. Stochastic volatility models must be designed with the robustness to identify and mitigate the influence of such manipulative activities on volatility estimates.

Example: Implementing anomaly detection algorithms within the model can help identify patterns indicative of manipulative practices. Once detected, these can be factored out or adjusted for in the volatility calculations, enhancing the model's reliability.

Adapting models for HFT also involves navigating ethical

considerations and compliance with regulatory standards. Models must not only be effective but also operate within the bounds of fair trading practices.

Example: This might involve incorporating mechanisms to ensure that the model's operations do not inadvertently result in market disruptions or unfair advantages. Regular audits and adherence to ethical AI practices can help maintain compliance and uphold market integrity.

Adapting stochastic volatility models for high-frequency trading environments presents a unique set of challenges and opportunities. From ensuring real-time data processing capabilities to maintaining ethical standards, each consideration plays a vital role in the model's success. As we push the envelope in HFT, the continuous refinement of these models in alignment with technological advancements and regulatory developments will be crucial for achieving superior trading performance and market stability.

CHAPTER 4: PYTHON FOR QUANTITATIVE FINANCE

Python has emerged as the lingua franca of financial modeling due to its simplicity, versatility, and the vast array of libraries it supports. For quantitative finance, certain libraries form the core of any analyst's toolkit:

- NumPy: Offers comprehensive mathematical functions, random number generators, linear algebra routines, Fourier transforms, and more.

- pandas: Provides high-performance, easy-to-use data structures, and data analysis tools.

- matplotlib: A plotting library for creating static, interactive, and animated visualizations in Python.

- SciPy: Used for scientific computing and technical computing.

- scikit-learn: For machine learning and statistical modeling including classification, regression, clustering, and dimensionality reduction.

- tensorflow/keras or pytorch: Advanced libraries for deep learning applications.

The journey begins with the installation of Python. While Python can be installed directly from python.org, a more convenient and widely adopted approach among data scientists and quants is to install Anaconda. Anaconda simplifies package management and deployment, offering a streamlined way to manage libraries and dependencies.

1. Anaconda Installation:

- Visit the Anaconda website and download the Anaconda Distribution for Python.

- Follow the installation prompts, ensuring that you opt to "Add Anaconda to my PATH environment variable" for ease of access from the command line.

2. Creating a Virtual Environment:

- Open your terminal (or Anaconda Prompt if on Windows).

- Create a new virtual environment by running: `conda create --name finance python=3.8`.

- Activate the environment with: `conda activate finance`.

3. Installing Core Libraries:

- With the environment activated, install the essential libraries by running: `conda install numpy pandas matplotlib scipy scikit-learn`.

4. Jupyter Notebooks:

- Jupyter notebooks offer an interactive coding experience, allowing you to execute Python code in a step-by-step manner. Install Jupyter by running: `conda install jupyter`.

- Launch Jupyter Notebook by typing: `jupyter notebook` in your terminal. This will open Jupyter in your default web browser, ready for coding.

- Version Control: It is wise to keep track of the library versions you are using, especially for projects that will be shared or worked on collaboratively. This can prevent compatibility issues and ensure reproducibility of results.

- Environment Export: Anaconda allows you to export your environment settings with `conda list --export > environment.yml`. This is invaluable for sharing environments or setting up identical environments on different machines.

- Regular Updates: Libraries are regularly updated with new features and bug fixes. Keeping your environment updated with `conda update --all` ensures you have the latest tools at your disposal.

Setting up your Python environment can sometimes be a trial, with issues ranging from conflicting library versions to PATH environment variables not being set correctly. When trouble arises, the Python and Anaconda communities are invaluable resources. Platforms such as Stack Overflow and GitHub issues can also offer solutions and advice from fellow developers who may have faced similar challenges.

With your Python environment configured, you stand on the threshold of the vast and world of stochastic volatility modeling. The tools and libraries at your disposal are akin to the instruments of an orchestra, ready to be orchestrated into symphonies of financial analysis and predictive modeling. The subsequent sections will delve into the application of these tools, transforming theoretical knowledge into practical expertise.

Overview of Python and its Ecosystem for Scientific Computing

Python's design philosophy emphasizes code readability and syntax simplicity, facilitating the swift development of applications. This inherent simplicity, however, belies its powerful capabilities, especially when leveraged with an array of specialized libraries designed for scientific computing. The ecosystem surrounding Python is its greatest asset, comprising libraries that cater to diverse needs - from numerical computations and statistical analysis to machine learning and data visualization.

1. NumPy: The bedrock of numerical computing in Python. NumPy extends Python with support for large, multi-dimensional arrays and matrices, alongside a vast collection of high-level mathematical functions to operate on these arrays. Its efficiency and computational speed are unparalleled,

making it indispensable for data-intensive tasks.

2. pandas: Built on top of NumPy, pandas introduce data frames and series, making data manipulation and analysis more intuitive and efficient. Its ability to seamlessly handle time-series data, perform aggregations, and its extensive functionalities for data filtering, transformation, and visualization make it a stalwart in financial data analysis.

3. matplotlib: Visualization is crucial in scientific computing for data exploration, hypothesis testing, and presenting findings. matplotlib offers a comprehensive suite of plotting tools that are both powerful and flexible, enabling the creation of a wide range of static, animated, and interactive visualizations.

4. SciPy: Specializing in mathematical routines, SciPy builds upon NumPy and provides a collection of algorithms for optimization, integration, interpolation, eigenvalue problems, algebraic equations, differential equations, and many other tasks related to scientific computing.

5. scikit-learn: For predictive data analysis, scikit-learn offers simple and efficient tools for data mining and data analysis. It is built on NumPy, SciPy, and matplotlib, providing a consistent and accessible interface to a wide range of machine learning algorithms.

6. Jupyter Notebooks: Beyond libraries, the Python ecosystem encompasses tools like Jupyter Notebooks, which provide a web-based interactive computational environment. Here, code, visualizations, and narrative text are combined, making it a favored tool for data exploration, documentation, and

sharing of insights within the scientific community.

In quantitative finance, the integration of these components facilitates a comprehensive approach to financial modeling. For example, NumPy's array operations can simulate asset price paths, pandas can handle historical market data, matplotlib can visualize trading strategies' performance, and SciPy's optimization algorithms can calibrate model parameters to market data. Meanwhile, scikit-learn's machine learning capabilities enable the identification of complex patterns in financial markets, and Jupyter Notebooks serve as the platform where all these analyses are documented and shared.

While Python's ecosystem offers unparalleled advantages, it is not without its challenges. Performance optimization, especially for large-scale simulations and real-time analytics, requires a deep understanding of these libraries and efficient coding practices. Additionally, the interdependencies between libraries necessitate staying updated with the latest versions to avoid compatibility issues.

The Python ecosystem for scientific computing is a testament to the language's adaptability and the collaborative spirit of its community. For those venturing into the quantitative finance landscape, mastering this ecosystem not only provides the tools necessary for sophisticated financial modeling but also opens doors to innovative research and development opportunities in this ever-evolving field.

Important Libraries: NumPy, pandas, matplotlib, SciPy

NumPy, short for Numerical Python, is the foundational

package for scientific computing in Python. It provides support for arrays, matrices, and a large library of high-level mathematical functions to operate on these data structures. Its significance lies in its ability to perform complex mathematical operations with high efficiency and speed. For quantitative analysts, NumPy is indispensable for tasks such as:

- Generating simulations or models of financial markets.

- Performing statistical analysis and mathematical operations on large datasets.

- Building and backtesting trading strategies with speed and precision.

pandas stands out for its easy-to-use data structures and data analysis tools. The library's main feature, the DataFrame, enables data manipulation with integrated indexing for quick data slicing, reshaping, and aggregating. In finance, pandas is particularly useful for:

- Handling time-series data, crucial for financial analysis involving stock prices, economic indicators, and other time-dependent data.

- Cleaning, transforming, and analyzing financial datasets to derive actionable insights.

- Merging and joining disparate data sources into a coherent dataset for analysis.

matplotlib is a powerful plotting library that allows for the creation of static, animated, and interactive visualizations in Python. It is incredibly versatile, enabling the visualization of data in a format that is most useful for the task at hand. In quantitative finance, matplotlib is used for:

- Charting historical stock prices or financial indicators to identify trends and patterns.

- Visualizing the outcomes of trading strategies or models to assess their performance.

- Creating dashboards of financial metrics to monitor the health of investments or portfolios.

SciPy builds on the capabilities of NumPy and provides additional functionality for optimization, integration, interpolation, and other tasks essential in scientific computing. Its algorithms are engineered for efficiency and reliability, making it a go-to library for quantitative finance applications such as:

- Optimizing investment portfolios to maximize returns or minimize risk.

- Modeling and pricing complex financial instruments using differential equations and other mathematical models.

- Conducting statistical tests to validate trading strategies or financial models.

While each of these libraries is powerful on its own, combining them unlocks new potentials. For instance, one might use NumPy arrays for efficient numerical operations, pandas for data manipulation, matplotlib for visualization, and SciPy for applying scientific methods to the data. This synergy allows for the development of sophisticated financial models and strategies with a level of ease and efficiency that was not possible before.

The integration of NumPy, pandas, matplotlib, and SciPy into Python's ecosystem provides a potent toolkit for anyone venturing into the domain of quantitative finance. Their combined capabilities allow for tackling almost any challenge in financial analysis, from the simplest data visualization task to the most complex numerical simulation. As we continue to explore the applications of these libraries in subsequent sections, it will become evident how they serve as the building blocks for advanced financial models and strategies.

Basics of Python Programming for Finance

Python's ascendancy in the financial domain is attributable to its simplicity and versatility. Its syntax is intuitive, making it accessible for newcomers yet powerful enough for complex analysis and model development. The ecosystem of libraries such as NumPy for numerical computing, pandas for data manipulation, matplotlib for data visualization, and many others, provides a robust framework for financial data analysis and modeling.

- Data Types and Structures: Understanding Python's basic data types (integers, floats, strings) and advanced structures (lists, tuples, dictionaries, and sets) is crucial. Financial data analysis involves manipulating various types of data, and these structures provide the foundational elements for data organization and manipulation.

- Control Flow: Conditional statements (if, elif, else) and loops (for, while) are essential for creating algorithms that can process financial data, from simple data cleaning tasks to complex model simulations.

- Functions and Modules: Decomposing code into reusable functions and organizing it within modules enhances code readability, maintainability, and modularity. This is particularly useful in financial modeling, where complex calculations are routine.

- NumPy: numerical computing in Python, NumPy offers efficient array operations and mathematical functions that underpin many financial calculations, from simple statistics to complex numerical simulations.

- pandas: This library is a powerhouse for financial data analysis, providing flexible data structures (Series and DataFrame) that facilitate efficient manipulation, aggregation, and visualization of financial datasets.

- matplotlib: A fundamental tool for data visualization, matplotlib enables the creation of a wide range of static, interactive, and animated plots and charts that are essential for data exploration and presentation of financial insights.

- Data Retrieval: Fetching data is the first step in financial analysis. Python's ecosystem includes libraries like `requests` for HTTP requests to access web-based financial data and `pandas-datareader` for importing data from a variety of financial platforms.

- Data Cleaning and Preparation: Real-world financial data is often messy. Using pandas, one can efficiently handle missing values, duplicate data, and data type conversions to prepare datasets for analysis.

- Numerical Analysis and Modeling: With NumPy and SciPy, financial practitioners can perform complex numerical analyses, such as optimization algorithms, linear algebra operations, and statistical analyses, that are central to financial modeling.

- Vectorization: Utilize NumPy's vectorized operations to enhance computational efficiency. Vectorization can significantly speed up data processing tasks, a critical factor in financial applications dealing with large datasets.

- Modularization: Develop modular code by organizing related functions and classes into modules and packages. This practice not only enhances code reuse but also simplifies maintenance and collaboration.

- Version Control: Employ version control tools, notably Git, along with platforms like GitHub, to manage code changes, collaborate on projects, and ensure reproducibility of analyses.

Mastering the basics of Python programming paves the way for financial analysts to dive into the multifaceted world of quantitative finance. The convergence of Python's intuitive programming paradigm with its comprehensive ecosystem of libraries creates an unparalleled platform for financial analysis and modeling. As we transition from foundational programming concepts to their application in finance, the ensuing sections will explore the development and implementation of specific financial models and strategies, underpinned by the Python skills delineated herein. This journey through Python for finance is not merely about acquiring technical proficiency but embracing a computational mindset essential for innovation and analysis in the financial domain.

Introduction to Python Syntax and Basic Programming Concepts

Python's syntax is renowned for its clarity and simplicity, making it an ideal language for beginners and experts alike. Python emphasizes readability, allowing programmers to express concepts without the verbose code seen in other languages. Here's an overview of the key aspects of Python syntax that form the foundation of programming in this language:

- Indentation: Unlike many other programming languages that use braces to define blocks of code, Python uses indentation. A consistent indent, typically four spaces, is crucial for delineating code blocks within functions, loops, and conditionals. This feature not only enhances code readability but also enforces a neat structure to your programming logic.

- Comments: Comments are essential for adding descriptive text to your code, making it more readable and maintainable. In Python, a comment starts with a `#` symbol and extends to the end of the line. Multi-line comments can be created using triple quotes (`"""` or `'''`), although technically, these are multi-line strings.

- Variables and Data Types: Python is dynamically typed, which means you don't need to declare the data type of a variable when you create one. Variables are assigned with a simple `=` operator, and Python infers the data type automatically. Understanding the built-in data types such as integers (`int`), floating-point numbers (`float`), strings (`str`), and booleans (`bool`) is pivotal for data manipulation in financial analysis.

- Basic Operators: Python supports a wide range of operators for performing mathematical calculations (`+`, `-`, `*`, `/`), logical operations (`and`, `or`, `not`), and comparisons (`==`, `!=`, `<`, `>`, `<=`, `>=`). Mastering these operators is fundamental for creating both simple and complex financial models.

To harness Python's full potential in financial applications, it's imperative to grasp the core constructs that govern the flow of execution in a program:

- Conditional Statements: `if`, `elif`, and `else` statements allow you to execute different blocks of code based on certain conditions. These are invaluable for implementing decision-making logic in financial algorithms.

- Loops: Python provides `for` and `while` loops, enabling repetitive execution of a block of code. Whether iterating over financial data points or calculating compounded interest, loops are indispensable.

- Functions: Functions are self-contained modules of code

that perform a specific task. In Python, functions are defined using the `def` keyword. Understanding how to create and use functions is crucial for modularizing your code, making it more organized and reusable.

With the basics of Python syntax and core programming constructs at your fingertips, you're well-prepared to dive deeper into the practical aspects of Python in finance. The subsequent sections will introduce you to more advanced concepts and libraries that enable data analysis, financial modeling, and algorithmic trading. Remember, mastery of Python for finance begins with a strong foundation in these fundamental programming principles. Each concept discussed here serves as a stepping stone towards becoming proficient in financial programming with Python, setting the stage for exploring complex financial models and strategies that will be covered in detail as we progress through the book.

Data Structures: Lists, Tuples, and Dictionaries for Financial Data

In Python, lists are akin to dynamic arrays that can contain items of varying data types. They are ordered, mutable, and encapsulate the essence of sequence data structures. For financial analysis, lists prove invaluable for their versatility and functionality. Consider a scenario where you're tracking the daily closing prices of a particular stock. A list allows you to store these prices in a sequential manner, enabling easy access and manipulation.

- Creating and Accessing Lists: Initializing a list is straightforward, using square brackets `[]` with items separated by commas. Accessing elements is done via indexing, starting at zero. For instance, `closing_prices[0]` retrieves the first closing price in your list.

- List Operations: Lists support a myriad of operations such as appending new items (`append()`), removing items (`remove()`), and slicing, which is particularly useful for time-series data manipulation in finance.

Tuples, much like lists, are ordered sequences of items. The critical difference lies in their immutability; once a tuple is created, its content cannot be changed. This feature makes tuples an excellent choice for storing financial data that shouldn't be altered, such as a set of fixed attributes for a financial instrument, e.g., (`'AAPL'`, `119.26`, `'USD'`), representing a stock symbol, price, and currency.

- Efficiency and Use Cases: Due to their immutable nature, tuples are more memory-efficient than lists. They are widely used to represent rows from database queries or fixed data points in financial models, ensuring data integrity and preventing accidental modifications.

Dictionaries are Python's built-in mapping type, characterized by their key-value pair structure. This data structure is optimized for retrieving data and is indispensable for financial analysis where you need to associate values with unique identifiers. For example, a dictionary could be used to map stock symbols to their respective closing prices, offering $O(1)$ lookup time for any given symbol.

- Advantages in Financial Computing: The direct association between keys and values allows for organizing complex financial datasets in a structured manner. Whether it's mapping ticker symbols to stock data or associating dates with financial events, dictionaries provide a highly efficient and readable means to manage financial information.

- Manipulation and Access: Accessing and setting values in dictionaries is straightforward, utilizing the `dict[key]` notation. Methods like `keys()`, `values()`, and `items()` offer flexible ways to iterate over dictionaries, which is particularly useful in financial calculations and data analysis scripts.

Mastering lists, tuples, and dictionaries, financial analysts and Python developers can significantly enhance their ability to process and analyze financial data. These structures serve as the building blocks for more complex data manipulation and analysis tasks, such as constructing financial models, back-testing trading strategies, and performing statistical analyses on financial time series. Their proper application not only streamlines data management tasks but also opens the door to deeper insights and more innovative financial solutions.

Understanding and effectively utilizing these data structures are fundamental steps towards achieving proficiency in financial programming with Python. As the complexity of financial data and the sophistication of analysis techniques continue to grow, the power and flexibility of Python's data structures become ever more critical tools in the financial analyst's toolkit.

Reading, Processing, and Visualizing Financial Data with Pandas and Matplotlib

Pandas, a library developed specifically for data manipulation and analysis, offers an intuitive interface for handling financial time series data. Its DataFrame object is a powerhouse, capable of storing and manipulating structured data with ease. Here's how pandas revolutionizes the way financial data is processed:

- Reading Data: Pandas supports reading data from various sources — CSVs, Excel files, databases, and even directly from financial data APIs. The `read_csv()` function, for instance, allows analysts to import historical stock price data with just a single line of code, transforming it into a manipulable DataFrame.

- Data Cleaning and Preparation: Financial datasets often come with their own set of challenges, including missing values, duplicate entries, and irrelevant columns. Pandas provides a comprehensive toolkit for cleaning data, including functions like `dropna()`, `drop_duplicates()`, and `fillna()`, ensuring that the dataset is primed for analysis.

- Time-Series Data Manipulation: With pandas, dealing with dates and times is straightforward. Its powerful time-series functionality allows for indexing by date/time, resampling for different time periods, and shifting/lagging of time series, which are critical operations in financial analysis.

Matplotlib complements pandas by bringing the processed data to life through visualization. It provides a robust plotting library capable of creating a wide range of static, interactive, and animated visualizations. Here's how matplotlib serves as an essential tool for financial data visualization:

- Plotting Time Series: Matplotlib excels in plotting time series data, such as stock price movements over time. Using the `plot()` function, analysts can effortlessly generate line graphs to visualize trends, patterns, and volatility in financial markets.

- Customizable Plots: The library offers extensive customization options, from adjusting colors and labels to configuring axes and grids. This flexibility is crucial for tailoring visualizations to specific analytical needs or presentation standards in finance.

- Advanced Financial Charts: Beyond basic plots, matplotlib can create sophisticated financial charts, such as candlestick and OHLC (Open-High-Low-Close) charts. These charts are indispensable tools for traders and analysts, providing deep insights into market sentiment and price movements.

The true power of pandas and matplotlib is unlocked when used in tandem. Here's a concise example that illustrates the synergy between these libraries:

```python
import pandas as pd

import matplotlib.pyplot as plt

# Reading stock price data into a pandas DataFrame

stock_data = pd.read_csv('AAPL.csv', parse_dates=True, index_col='Date')
```

```
# Processing data: Calculating the moving average

stock_data['MA50']                                          =
stock_data['Close'].rolling(window=50).mean()

# Visualizing the stock's closing price and moving average

plt.figure(figsize=(10,6))

plt.plot(stock_data['Close'], label='AAPL Close', color='blue')

plt.plot(stock_data['MA50'], label='50-Day Moving Average',
color='red')

plt.title('AAPL Stock Price and Moving Average')

plt.xlabel('Date')

plt.ylabel('Price')

plt.legend()

plt.show()

` ` `
```

This example succinctly demonstrates how to read, process, and visualize financial data, showcasing the closing prices of Apple's stock along with its 50-day moving average.

Such analyses are invaluable in identifying trends, support and resistance levels, and potential buying or selling opportunities.

The integration of pandas for data manipulation and matplotlib for visualization provides a formidable toolkit for financial analysts. By mastering these libraries, one can efficiently process vast amounts of financial data and visualize complex market dynamics. This synergy not only sharpens analytical skills but also unveils opportunities and risks within financial markets, guiding strategic investment decisions. As we continue to navigate the world of financial data, the proficiency in these Python libraries will undoubtedly remain a cornerstone for successful financial analysis.

Object-Oriented Programming for Financial Models

Understanding the four fundamental pillars of OOP is crucial for leveraging its full potential in financial models:

- Encapsulation: This principle involves bundling the data (attributes) and methods (functions) that operate on the data into a single unit, or class. Encapsulation offers a way to restrict access to certain components of an object, preventing accidental modification or misuse.

- Inheritance: Inheritance allows a new class to inherit attributes and methods from an existing class. This is particularly useful in financial modeling for building a hierarchy of model components, reducing redundancy, and enhancing the model's modularity.

- Polymorphism: Polymorphism enables a single interface to represent different underlying forms (data types). In finance, this allows the same operations to be applied to different financial instruments, such as stocks and bonds, through a common interface, facilitating code reusability and flexibility.

- Abstraction: Abstraction simplifies complex reality by modeling classes appropriate to the problem, and not dealing with the unnecessary details. In financial models, this means representing complex market behaviors with simplified, yet sufficiently accurate, models.

To illustrate these principles, let's construct a basic class for a stochastic process, a foundational concept in constructing financial models like the Black-Scholes or Heston model for option pricing.

```python
import numpy as np

class StochasticProcess:

    def __init__(self, mu=0, sigma=1, start_price=100):

        self.mu = mu

        self.sigma = sigma

        self.start_price = start_price
```

```python
def generate_price_path(self, time_steps=100, dt=1):

    """Generates a price path for the stochastic process."""

    prices = [self.start_price]

    for _ in range(1, time_steps):

        prices.append(prices[-1] + self.mu*dt + self.sigma*np.sqrt(dt)*np.random.normal())

    return prices
```

```

In this `StochasticProcess` class, `mu` represents the drift (mean return), `sigma` the volatility of the process, and `start_price` the initial price of the financial instrument. The `generate_price_path` method simulates a price path based on the specified parameters, illustrating encapsulation by bundling data and operations within the class.

Utilizing inheritance, we can extend this basic class to simulate more complex stochastic processes, such as the Heston model, which incorporates stochastic volatility into the price path simulation.

```python
class HestonProcess(StochasticProcess):
```
```

```
def __init__(self, mu, sigma, start_price, kappa, theta, xi, rho):

    super().__init__(mu, sigma, start_price)

    self.kappa = kappa  # Rate at which volatility reverts to theta

    self.theta = theta  # Long-term volatility mean

    self.xi = xi      # Volatility of volatility

    self.rho = rho    # Correlation between asset price and volatility


    # Additional methods to implement the Heston model
    specifics could be added here


```
```

This `HestonProcess` class inherits from `StochasticProcess` and adds new parameters to model stochastic volatility, demonstrating inheritance. The ability to extend and modify classes without altering the base class underscores the power of OOP in building adaptable financial models.

Object-Oriented Programming offers a structured and intuitive approach to constructing financial models, aligning with the complexity and hierarchical nature of financial instruments and markets. By encapsulating data and behavior into classes, leveraging inheritance for model component hierarchies, and employing polymorphism and abstraction,
```

OOP facilitates the development of flexible, modular, and scalable financial models. The Python examples provided here serve as a foundation, illustrating how financial analysts and quants can implement OOP principles to model the behaviors of financial markets effectively.

The Concept of Classes and Objects in Python

A class in Python acts as a blueprint for creating objects. It defines a set of attributes and methods that characterize any object instantiated from the class. Attributes are data members (class variables and instance variables) that store data specific to each object. Methods, on the other hand, are functions defined within a class that operate on the attributes of the objects, defining their behavior.

```python
class FinancialInstrument:

# Class variable

instrument_type = "Generic Financial Instrument"

# The __init__ method acts as a constructor

def __init__(self, symbol, price):

self.symbol = symbol  # Instance variable

self.price = price   # Instance variable
```

```python
# Method to update price

def update_price(self, new_price):

    self.price = new_price

    print(f"The new price of {self.symbol} is {self.price}")
```

```

```

In this example, `FinancialInstrument` is a class with a class variable `instrument_type`, two instance variables `symbol` and `price`, and a method `update_price`. The class serves as a generic template for financial instruments, encapsulating properties and behaviors common to various instruments.

Objects are instances of a class, created to represent individual entities conforming to the class blueprint. When an object is instantiated, it inherits all the attributes and methods defined in the class, allowing for the manipulation of data specific to the object.

```python

# Creating objects from the FinancialInstrument class

stock = FinancialInstrument("AAPL", 150)

bond = FinancialInstrument("US0323XAE21", 105)
```

Updating and printing the price of the stock

stock.update_price(155)

```
` ` `
```

In this snippet, `stock` and `bond` are objects of the `FinancialInstrument` class, each representing a different financial instrument with unique symbols and prices. The method `update_price` is called on the `stock` object, demonstrating how methods defined in the class blueprint can manipulate data within individual objects.

Polymorphism in Python allows for methods to be used in a manner that is agnostic to the object's class type, provided that the method signatures are compatible. This enables flexibility and reuse of code, as seen in the following extension of our financial modeling context.

```python
class Stock(FinancialInstrument):

def update_price(self, new_price):

# Specific implementation for a stock

self.price = new_price - new_price * 0.02  # Applying a discount

print(f"Stock price updated with discount: {self.price}")
```

```
# Polymorphism in action

instruments = [stock, bond]

for instrument in instruments:

    instrument.update_price(120)

```

Here, `Stock` is a subclass of `FinancialInstrument` with an overridden `update_price` method, illustrating polymorphism. The loop at the end updates the price of both stocks and bonds using their respective `update_price` implementations, showcasing how one interface (`update_price`) can adapt to the form of the underlying object (`stock` or `bond`).

Building a Basic Stochastic Process Class

A stochastic process, represents a sequence of random variables evolving over time. To encapsulate this in Python, we commence by defining a class that mirrors these characteristics. The goal is to create a flexible, reusable class that can simulate various stochastic processes, including but not limited to the geometric Brownian motion often applied in finance.

```python
```

```python
import numpy as np

class StochasticProcess:

    def __init__(self, initial_value=0):

        self.initial_value = initial_value

        self.path = [initial_value]

    def simulate_path(self, time_steps=100, drift=0, volatility=1):

        for _ in range(time_steps):

            random_step = np.random.normal(loc=drift, scale=volatility)

            new_value = self.path[-1] + random_step

            self.path.append(new_value)

        return self.path

```

In the core structure of the `StochasticProcess` class, the constructor initializes the process with an `initial_value`. The `simulate_path` method, pivotal to the class, generates a path of values over specified `time_steps`. This simulation leverages the `numpy` library to inject randomness, mimicking the stochastic nature of market movements.

To amplify the class's utility, we incorporate methods allowing for parameter adjustments, enabling the simulation of a wide array of stochastic processes under different conditions.

```python
def reset_path(self):

self.path = [self.initial_value]

def    update_parameters(self,    new_initial_value=None,
new_drift=None, new_volatility=None):

if new_initial_value is not None:

self.initial_value = new_initial_value

self.reset_path()

if new_drift is not None:

self.drift = new_drift

if new_volatility is not None:

self.volatility = new_volatility
```

` ` `

These additions empower users to reset the simulation path to its initial state or alter the process parameters, thereby enhancing the class's versatility in financial modeling scenarios.

To demonstrate the class's practical application, we simulate a geometric Brownian motion (GBM), a staple in modeling stock prices. GBM is characterized by a constant drift and volatility, making it an ideal candidate for our `StochasticProcess` class.

```python

class GBM(StochasticProcess):

def simulate_path(self, time_steps=100, drift=0.05, volatility=):

for _ in range(1, time_steps + 1):

dt = 1 / time_steps

random_step = np.random.normal(loc=0, scale=np.sqrt(dt))

new_value = self.path[-1] * np.exp((drift - * volatility 2) * dt + volatility * random_step)

self.path.append(new_value)
```

return self.path

` ` `

Inheriting from `StochasticProcess`, the `GBM` class tailors the path simulation to reflect the specific dynamics of geometric Brownian motion, showcasing the class's adaptability to diverse financial models.

With our basic stochastic process class in place, financial analysts and quants can now simulate and analyze a plethora of market scenarios. Whether evaluating risk, pricing derivatives, or crafting investment strategies, the class provides a robust foundation for stochastic modeling in Python.

- Simulate multiple paths to gauge potential future price ranges of assets.

- Integrate into Monte Carlo methods for option pricing or risk assessment.

- Experiment with various drift and volatility parameters to understand their impact on asset behavior.

The construction of a basic stochastic process class represents a significant stride towards demystifying the stochastic nature of financial markets. By bridging theoretical concepts with practical implementation, this class lays the groundwork for sophisticated financial modeling and analysis, empowering users to explore the stochastic underpinnings of markets with newfound precision and flexibility.

CHAPTER 5: BUILDING STOCHASTIC VOLATILITY MODELS IN PYTHON

The Euler-Maruyama method stands as a numerical approximation technique, specifically designed to address stochastic differential equations (SDEs) inherent in financial models like the Heston model. this method bridges the gap between the continuous stochastic processes described by SDEs and the discrete simulations required for computational finance.

Consider a general SDE constituting the evolution of a financial asset's price, S, represented as:

$$dS_t = \mu(S_t, t)dt + \sigma(S_t, t)dW_t$$

where $\mu(S_t, t)$ and $\sigma(S_t, t)$ denote the drift and volatility components, respectively, and W_t signifies a Wiener process.

The Euler-Maruyama approximation for this SDE, over a time step Δt, is given by:

$$S_{t+\Delta t} = S_t + \mu(S_t, t)\Delta t + \sigma(S_t, t)\sqrt{\Delta t}Z_t$$

where Z_t is a standard normal random variable.

A Python implementation of the Euler-Maruyama method to simulate price paths under the Heston model can be approached as follows:

```python
import numpy as np

# Parameters for the Heston model

mu = 0.05  # Drift

kappa = 2.0  # Rate of reversion

theta = 0.02  # Long-run variance

xi = 0.1  # Volatility of volatility

rho = -  # Correlation between asset and variance

V0 = 0.01  # Initial variance
```

```
S0 = 100  # Initial asset price

T = 1  # Time to maturity

dt = 1/252  # Daily time step

N = int(T/dt)  # Number of time steps

# Initializing the paths

S_path = np.zeros(N+1)

V_path = np.zeros(N+1)

S_path[0] = S0

V_path[0] = V0

# Standard normal random numbers

Z1 = np.random.normal(0, 1, N)

Z2 = rho*Z1 + np.sqrt(1-rho2)*np.random.normal(0, 1, N)

# Simulating the price path

for t in range(1, N+1):
```

```python
        V_t = np.maximum(V_path[t-1], 0)  # Ensure variance is non-negative

        S_path[t] = S_path[t-1] + mu*S_path[t-1]*dt + np.sqrt(V_t*dt)*Z1[t-1]

        V_path[t] = V_path[t-1] + kappa*(theta-V_t)*dt + xi*np.sqrt(V_t*dt)*Z2[t-1]

# Visualization

import matplotlib.pyplot as plt

plt.figure(figsize=(10, 6))

plt.plot(S_path, label='Asset Price')

plt.plot(V_path, label='Variance')

plt.title('Simulated Price Path using Euler-Maruyama')

plt.xlabel('Time Steps')

plt.ylabel('Price / Variance')

plt.legend()

plt.show()
```

```
` ` `
```

This implementation succinctly encapsulates the essence of the Euler-Maruyama method by discretizing both the asset price and variance paths under the Heston model's framework. The choice of parameters and the method's inherent assumptions must be tailored to align with the specific characteristics of the financial instrument in question.

The simulated price paths are instrumental in option pricing, particularly within the Monte Carlo simulation framework. By generating a multitude of possible future paths for the underlying asset, one can calculate the option's payoff under each scenario and subsequently average these payoffs, discounting back to present value. This approach allows for the pricing of complex derivatives, for which closed-form solutions may not exist.

Simulating price paths embodies a fundamental technique in quantitative finance, pivotal for both strategic analysis and derivative pricing. The Euler-Maruyama method, exemplified within the Heston model, offers a pragmatic approach to tackling the complexities of stochastic volatility. The meticulously crafted Python code serves as a tangible guide for practitioners, encapsulating the theoretical concepts into actionable insights. This amalgamation of theory and practice equips finance professionals with the necessary tools to navigate the multifaceted landscape of financial markets, harnessing the predictive power of stochastic processes to forge innovative trading strategies.

The Euler-Maruyama Method for Simulating SDEs

The Euler-Maruyama method is anchored in the principle of discretizing continuous stochastic processes, thereby making the complex landscape of SDEs more tractable for computational analysis. It provides a gateway to approximating the solutions of SDEs, which are often analytically intractable due to their inherent randomness components.

Consider an SDE delineated as:

$$ dX_t = a(X_t, t)dt + b(X_t, t)dW_t $$

where X_t symbolizes the stochastic process of interest, $(a(X_t, t))$ and $(b(X_t, t))$ represent the drift and diffusion coefficients respectively, and dW_t signifies the increments of a Wiener process.

The Euler-Maruyama approximation posits that for a small timestep Δt, the process X_t evolves as:

$$ X_{t+\Delta t} = X_t + a(X_t, t)\Delta t + b(X_t, t)\sqrt{\Delta t}Z $$

where Z is drawn from a standard normal distribution, encapsulating the stochastic increment.

Implementing the Euler-Maruyama method in Python serves as a practical conduit to simulate SDEs, thereby enabling the visualization and analysis of their behavior. Following is a nuanced Python implementation, enhancing the previous example by focusing on the method's adaptability to various

SDEs:

```python
import numpy as np

import matplotlib.pyplot as plt

# Function defining the SDE's coefficients

def a(x, t):

return kappa * (theta - x)

def b(x, t):

return xi * np.sqrt(np.maximum(x, 0))

# Time parameters

T = 1

dt = 1/252

N = int(T/dt)

t = np.linspace(0, T, N+1)

# Initial condition
```

```
X0 = V0

# Simulating the process

X_path = np.zeros(N+1)

X_path[0] = X0

Z = np.random.normal(0, 1, N)

for i in range(1, N+1):

X_path[i]    =    X_path[i-1]    +    a(X_path[i-1],    t[i-1])*dt    +
b(X_path[i-1], t[i-1])*np.sqrt(dt)*Z[i-1]

# Plotting the simulated path

plt.figure(figsize=(10, 6))

plt.plot(t, X_path, label='Simulated Process')

plt.title('SDE Simulation using Euler-Maruyama')

plt.xlabel('Time')

plt.ylabel('Process Value')

plt.legend()
```

```
plt.show()

` ` `
```

This snippet elucidates the flexibility of the Euler-Maruyama method in simulating a generic SDE by abstracting the drift and diffusion functions. The choice of parameters and functions `a` and `b` can be adjusted to simulate a wide array of stochastic processes, illustrating the method's versatility.

While the Euler-Maruyama method provides a robust framework for SDE simulation, its fidelity hinges on the granularity of the timestep Δt and the specific characteristics of the process being modeled. The method's simplicity and computational efficiency make it a stalwart choice for preliminary simulations. However, one must be cognizant of its limitations, particularly in scenarios with significant non-linearity or in the presence of strong drift or diffusion components.

The Euler-Maruyama method, with its theoretical elegance and practical utility, stands as a bulwark in the quantitative finance domain for simulating SDEs. Its Pythonic implementation not only demystifies the stochastic calculus involved but also empowers practitioners with the capability to visualize, analyze, and leverage the stochastic nature of financial markets. As we delve deeper into the realms of stochastic volatility and financial modeling, the insights gleaned from such simulations become indispensable, guiding the development of nuanced trading strategies and risk management practices.

Implementing the Monte Carlo Simulation for the Heston Model

Central to the Heston model is the notion that volatility itself follows a stochastic process, described by the following set of stochastic differential equations (SDEs):

$$ dS_t = \mu S_t \, dt + \sqrt{v_t} \, S_t \, dW_t^S $$

$$ dv_t = \kappa (\theta - v_t) \, dt + \xi \sqrt{v_t} \, dW_t^v $$

Here, S_t represents the asset price, v_t denotes the stochastic volatility, μ is the rate of return, κ measures the speed of reversion to the mean volatility θ, and ξ is the volatility of the volatility. dW_t^S and dW_t^v are Wiener processes that may be correlated.

Monte Carlo simulations generate numerous paths for the underlying variables by random sampling, thus enabling the estimation of derivatives prices as averages over these paths. These simulations are particularly potent for models like Heston's, where analytical solutions might be complex or infeasible.

A Python script to simulate asset paths under the Heston model involves generating two correlated Brownian motions to reflect the correlation between the asset price and its volatility. The complexity of the Heston model necessitates careful numerical techniques to ensure stability and accuracy:

```python
```

```python
import numpy as np

import matplotlib.pyplot as plt

# Model parameters

S0 = 100     # Initial asset price

V0 = 0.04    # Initial volatility

kappa = 1.5  # Speed of reversion

theta = 0.04 # Long-term volatility

xi = 0.1     # Volatility of volatility

rho = -    # Correlation between asset and volatility

T = 1        # Time to maturity

mu = 0.05    # Asset expected return

N = 365      # Number of time steps

M = 1000     # Number of simulation paths

dt = T/N     # Time step size
```

```
np.random.seed(0)  # Set the seed for reproducibility

def simulate_heston_model():

dt_sqrt = np.sqrt(dt)

S = np.zeros((N+1, M))

V = np.zeros((N+1, M))

S[0] = S0

V[0] = V0

# Generating correlated Brownian motions

W_S = np.random.normal(0, 1, (N+1, M))

W_V = rho * W_S + np.sqrt(1 - rho2) * np.random.normal(0, 1,
(N+1, M))

for t in range(1, N+1):

# Ensuring volatility stays non-negative

V[t] = np.maximum(V[t-1] + kappa * (theta - V[t-1]) * dt + xi *
np.sqrt(V[t-1]) * dt_sqrt * W_V[t], 0)
```

```python
S[t] = S[t-1] * np.exp((mu -  * V[t-1]) * dt + np.sqrt(V[t-1]) * dt_sqrt * W_S[t])

    return S, V

S, V = simulate_heston_model()

# Plotting a few paths

plt.figure(figsize=(14, 7))

for i in range(10):

    plt.plot(S[:, i])

plt.title('Simulated Asset Paths under the Heston Model')

plt.xlabel('Time Steps')

plt.ylabel('Asset Price')

plt.show()

# Volatility paths can also be plotted similarly to visualize the stochastic volatility behavior.

```
```
```

This code segment encapsulates the essence of the Heston model's implementation in a Monte Carlo simulation context, illustrating both the model's complexity and its capability to capture the dynamics of financial markets. Leveraging NumPy for vectorized operations ensures efficiency, enabling the simulation of thousands of paths swiftly.

The implementation of the Heston model via the Monte Carlo method in Python elucidates the practical mechanisms through which stochastic volatility can be modeled and analyzed. This methodology is indispensable for pricing complex derivatives, conducting risk management, and designing strategic trading algorithms. The insights garnered from such simulations underpin a deeper understanding of market dynamics, facilitating informed decision-making in the volatile realm of financial markets.

Visualization of Simulated Paths and Analysis

Effective visualization is paramount for interpreting the complex data generated by Monte Carlo simulations. Python, with its robust libraries such as Matplotlib and Seaborn, provides a versatile toolkit for crafting insightful visual representations:

1. Line Plots for Asset and Volatility Paths: Line plots are instrumental in depicting the evolution of asset prices and volatility over time. These plots can highlight the variance in paths that the stochastic process generates, offering a visual understanding of volatility clustering and extreme event probabilities.

2. Histograms of Final Asset Prices: By plotting the distribution of the final asset prices across all simulations, investors can gauge the potential outcomes of their investments. This histogram can reveal the skewness and kurtosis of returns, critical factors for risk assessment.

3. Volatility Surface: A more advanced visualization, the volatility surface plots implied volatilities on a three-dimensional surface against strike price and expiration time. This visualization can be particularly revealing for options traders, as it showcases the volatility smile or smirk that results from market imperfections.

4. Heatmaps of Correlation: Given the Heston model accounts for correlation between asset prices and their volatilities, a heatmap can succinctly display how these correlations fluctuate over time, providing insights into the co-movements of market variables.

To actualize these visualizations, the following Python snippet extends the earlier Monte Carlo simulation example, focusing on asset path and volatility visualization:

```python

import seaborn as sns

# Assuming S and V are the asset and volatility paths from the previous section

# Plotting the final asset prices' distribution
```

```
plt.figure(figsize=(10, 6))

sns.histplot(S[-1, :], kde=True, color='blue')

plt.title('Distribution of Final Asset Prices')

plt.xlabel('Asset Price')

plt.ylabel('Frequency')

plt.show()

# Volatility path for the first simulation

plt.figure(figsize=(14, 7))

plt.plot(V[:, 0])

plt.title('Volatility Path under the Heston Model')

plt.xlabel('Time Steps')

plt.ylabel('Volatility')

plt.show()

```
```
```

The visual analysis of simulated paths leads to several crucial insights:

- Understanding Volatility Clustering: Volatility clustering, a common market phenomenon, becomes evident through the visualization of volatility paths, offering a realistic depiction of market behavior.

- Risk Assessment: The distribution of final asset prices assists in understanding the risk associated with different investment strategies, particularly the tails of the distribution that represent extreme market movements.

- Strategic Decision Making: By analyzing the correlation between returns and volatility, traders can better strategize their hedge positions or identify arbitrage opportunities.

- Market Sentiment Analysis: The volatility surface can provide clues about market sentiment, especially in times of economic uncertainty or ahead of major announcements.

The adept visualization and analysis of simulated paths under the Heston model furnish traders and financial analysts with a profound understanding of market dynamics. This, in turn, enhances their ability to make informed decisions, devise robust trading strategies, and manage risk with greater precision. Through the meticulous examination of these visual representations, one can uncover nuanced insights into the stochastic behavior of financial markets, laying the groundwork for advanced trading and investment methodologies.

Option Pricing with Monte Carlo

Monte Carlo simulation for option pricing involves generating multiple scenarios for future asset price movements based on stochastic processes and calculating the option's payoff for each scenario. The option's price is then estimated as the average of these payoffs, discounted back to the present value. This method is particularly effective for pricing options where the payoff is path-dependent, such as Asian options, or for options on assets with stochastic volatility models.

The flexibility of Monte Carlo simulation allows for the modeling of complex derivatives and the incorporation of various features, such as early exercise provisions in American options, by simulating the optimal exercise strategy across the generated paths.

To implement Monte Carlo simulation for option pricing in Python, we leverage the power of libraries such as NumPy for numerical computation. The following example demonstrates the pricing of a European call option under the Black-Scholes framework using Monte Carlo simulation:

```python
import numpy as np

def monte_carlo_european_call_price(S0, K, T, r, sigma, M):

    """
```

Price a European call option using Monte Carlo simulation.

Parameters:

S0 : float - initial stock price

K : float - strike price

T : float - time to maturity

r : float - risk-free interest rate

sigma : float - volatility

M : int - number of simulations

Returns:

call_price : float - estimated price of the call option

"""

np.random.seed(42) # For reproducibility

dt = T # Time step

exp_term = np.exp(-r * T) # Discount factor

```
# Simulate end-of-period stock prices

ST = S0 * np.exp((r -  * sigma2) * dt + sigma * np.sqrt(dt) *
np.random.randn(M))

# Calculate payoffs and discount them back to present value

payoffs = np.maximum(ST - K, 0)

call_price = exp_term * np.mean(payoffs)

return call_price

# Example parameters

S0 = 100  # Initial stock price

K = 105  # Strike price

T = 1  # Time to maturity (in years)

r = 0.05  # Risk-free interest rate

sigma =   # Volatility

M = 10000  # Number of simulations

# Pricing the option
```

```
call_price = monte_carlo_european_call_price(S0, K, T, r,
sigma, M)

print(f"The estimated European call option price is: $
{call_price:.2f}")

` ` `
```

The Monte Carlo method's versatility extends beyond simple European options to more sophisticated financial instruments. However, its accuracy is contingent upon the number of simulated paths, with a higher number of simulations generally leading to more precise estimates. Computational efficiency, therefore, becomes a critical consideration, especially for real-time pricing and risk management.

Advanced techniques such as variance reduction methods (e.g., antithetic variates, control variates) and quasi-Monte Carlo methods can significantly enhance the efficiency and accuracy of Monte Carlo simulations. These methods are particularly valuable in a trading context, where speed and precision are paramount.

In summary, Monte Carlo simulation offers a powerful tool for option pricing, capable of accommodating complex payoffs and stochastic models. Its implementation in Python, illustrated above, underscores its accessibility to practitioners, enabling the development of sophisticated trading and risk management strategies. By mastering this technique, financial professionals can unlock new dimensions of financial modeling, paving the way for innovation and competitive advantage in the fast-paced world of finance.

Basics of Option Pricing Theory

An option is a financial derivative that grants the holder the right, but not the obligation, to buy or sell an underlying asset at a predetermined price, known as the strike price, within a specified time frame. The two primary types of options are calls and puts. A call option gives the holder the right to buy the underlying asset, while a put option confers the right to sell.

The intrinsic value of an option is determined by the relationship between the strike price and the current price of the underlying asset. However, the actual pricing of options goes beyond mere intrinsic value, incorporating the time value, which reflects the potential for the option to gain in value before its expiration. This amalgamation of intrinsic value and time value is where option pricing theory comes into play, bridging the gap between theoretical valuation and market reality.

The Black-Scholes model, introduced in 1973 by Fischer Black, Myron Scholes, and later expanded by Robert Merton, revolutionized option pricing by providing an analytical formula for valuing European options. The model operates under several assumptions:

- The stock price follows a geometric Brownian motion with constant drift and volatility.

- The risk-free rate is constant and known.

- No dividends are paid out during the life of the option.

- Markets are frictionless, with no transaction costs or taxes.

- The option can only be exercised at expiration (for European options).

The Black-Scholes formula for a European call option is given by:

$$C(S_0, K, T, r, \sigma) = S_0N(d_1) - Ke^{-rT}N(d_2)$$

where:

- S_0 is the current price of the underlying asset.

- K is the strike price.

- T is the time to expiration.

- r is the risk-free interest rate.

- σ is the volatility of the asset's returns.

- $N(\cdot)$ is the cumulative distribution function of the standard normal distribution.

- $d_1 = \frac{\ln(S_0/K) + (r + \sigma^2/2)T}{\sigma\sqrt{T}}$

- $d_2 = d_1 - \sigma\sqrt{T}$

While the Black-Scholes model laid the foundation for modern option pricing, financial markets' evolving complexity necessitated more nuanced models. The assumptions of the Black-Scholes model, particularly constant volatility and the inability to price American options (which can be exercised before expiration), led to the development of alternative models such as the Binomial Tree model and stochastic volatility models.

The Binomial Tree model, for instance, provides a flexible framework for valuing options with varying underlying asset dynamics and can accommodate American-style options. It prices options by constructing a lattice, or tree, of possible underlying asset prices over time, then calculates the option's value by iteratively determining the payoff at each node, working backward from expiration to the present.

Understanding the basics of option pricing theory is crucial for navigating the complex landscape of financial derivatives. The theories and models discussed serve as the bedrock upon which modern financial engineering is built, enabling practitioners to devise sophisticated trading and hedging strategies. As we delve deeper into stochastic volatility models and their implementation in Python in subsequent sections, the foundational knowledge of option pricing theory laid out here will prove invaluable, offering the conceptual tools necessary to grasp more advanced topics and applications in quantitative finance.

Pricing European and Exotic Options Under Stochastic Volatility

Stochastic volatility models introduce a revolutionary perspective by allowing the volatility of the underlying asset to be a stochastic process itself, in contrast to the constant volatility assumption in the Black-Scholes model. This adaptation captures the inherent volatility smiles and skews observed in the market, providing a more realistic modeling of financial instruments.

One of the seminal stochastic volatility models is the Heston model, which posits that volatility follows a mean-reverting square root process. The model's allure lies in its analytical tractability and the ability to produce closed-form solutions for European option prices, a rarity in complex models. The Heston model equation for a European call option, without delving into the mathematical depths, is an elegant testimony to the fusion of stochastic processes in option pricing.

The pricing of European options under the Heston model utilizes the characteristic function rather than direct pricing formulas. This approach, though mathematically intensive, yields a framework that adeptly prices options by considering the stochastic nature of volatility. The model's parameters, including the long-term mean volatility, volatility of volatility, and the rate of reversion, are calibrated from market data, providing a bespoke fit to market peculiarities.

For practitioners, the charm of the Heston model lies in its versatility and the richness it brings to option pricing. It allows for a nuanced understanding of how market conditions and volatility dynamics influence option prices, beyond the simplistic view of the Black-Scholes world.

The journey from European to exotic options under stochastic volatility is a leap from the classical to the vanguard of financial engineering. Exotic options, with their non-standard features and payoff structures, demand a pricing approach that transcends the conventional. Stochastic volatility models, with their malleable mathematical structure, extend a warm embrace to these complex instruments.

In the context of stochastic volatility, exotic options such as Asian, barrier, and lookback options are often priced using numerical methods like Monte Carlo simulations or finite difference methods. These methods, while computationally intensive, offer the flexibility to model the payoff patterns of exotic options and the stochastic nature of volatility simultaneously.

The practical implementation of the Heston model for pricing European and exotic options is facilitated by Python's rich ecosystem of libraries. Utilizing libraries such as NumPy for numerical computation, SciPy for optimization, and matplotlib for visualization, one can construct a Heston model simulator that calibrates to market data and prices options with stochastic volatility.

The following Python snippet outlines the essence of a Heston model implementation for pricing a European call option:

```python

import numpy as np

from scipy.stats import norm
```

```python
from scipy.optimize import minimize

def heston_call_price(kappa, theta, sigma, rho, v0, r, S0, K, T):

    # Define necessary functions for the Heston model
    implementation

    # This includes the characteristic function of the log stock
    price

    # and its integration to obtain the call price

    # Note: This is a simplified representation. Actual
    implementation

    # would involve complex calculations including Fourier
    transforms.

    # Placeholder for Heston model call price calculation

    call_price = "Call price calculation based on Heston model
    parameters"

    return call_price

# Example parameters (simplified)

kappa = 1.5  # Rate of reversion
```

```
theta = 0.04  # Long-term volatility

sigma =   # Volatility of volatility

rho = -   # Correlation between asset returns and volatility

v0 = 0.04  # Initial volatility

r = 0.05  # Risk-free rate

S0 = 100  # Current stock price

K = 100  # Strike price

T = 1  # Time to maturity (in years)

# Calculate European call option price

call_price = heston_call_price(kappa, theta, sigma, rho, v0, r, S0, K, T)

print(f"The European call option price under the Heston model is: {call_price}")

` ` `
```

Pricing European and exotic options under stochastic volatility embodies the confluence of theoretical finance and empirical observation. It provides a framework that appreciates the complexity of market behavior, offering tools that are both sophisticated and infinitely adaptable. As this exploration has shown, the journey through stochastic volatility models is not merely an academic endeavor but a practical voyage towards understanding and harnessing financial markets.

Efficiency Techniques: Antithetic Variates, Control Variates

The antithetic variates technique is a variance reduction method that leverages the concept of symmetry in random variable distributions. the method involves generating pairs of path samples where one sample in each pair is the "antithesis" or mirror image of the other in terms of their deviation from the mean. This approach effectively doubles the sample size without additional computational cost, leading to a more efficient estimation process.

For instance, in the context of a Monte Carlo simulation for option pricing, for every random path that suggests a possible future stock price trajectory, an antithetic path is generated by negating the random increments of the original path. The final option price estimate is then derived from the average of these paired samples.

Implementing antithetic variates in Python is straightforward, thanks to the language's comprehensive numerical libraries. The modification to a standard Monte Carlo simulation involves generating an additional set of paths with inverted signs for the stochastic components, and subsequently, averaging the results from both the original and antithetic paths.

```python

import numpy as np

def generate_antithetic_paths(S0, r, sigma, T, dt, N, M):

# S0: Initial stock price

# r: Risk-free rate

# sigma: Volatility

# T: Time to maturity

# dt: Time step size

# N: Number of time steps

# M: Number of paths

dt = T/N

t = np.linspace(0, T, N)

Z = np.random.normal(0, 1, (N, int(M/2)))

S = np.zeros((N, M))
```

```
S[0] = S0

for i in range(1, N):

S[i, :int(M/2)] = S[i-1, :int(M/2)] * np.exp((r -  * sigma2) * dt +
sigma * np.sqrt(dt) * Z[i-1])

S[i, int(M/2):] = S[i-1, int(M/2):] * np.exp((r -  * sigma2) * dt +
sigma * np.sqrt(dt) * -Z[i-1])

return S, t

# Example parameters

S0 = 100

r = 0.05

sigma =

T = 1

dt = 0.01

N = 100

M = 10000
```

```
S, t = generate_antithetic_paths(S0, r, sigma, T, dt, N, M)
```

```
` ` `
```

The control variates technique aims at reducing the variance of an estimator by exploiting the covariance between the estimator and a control variable with a known expected value. By adjusting the original estimator with a factor of the control variable, one can significantly reduce the estimator's variance, thereby enhancing the efficiency of simulations.

In practice, a common control variate for option pricing is the price of an option with a known analytical solution, such as a European call or put option under the Black-Scholes model. The difference between the Monte Carlo estimate and the known solution can be used to adjust the final estimate, reducing its variance.

The application of control variates within a Python-based Monte Carlo simulation involves calculating the control variate adjustment based on the covariance between the simulation outputs and the control, and the variance of the control itself.

```python
def control_variate_adjustment(mc_estimates, control_variates, control_variate_mean):

# mc_estimates: Monte Carlo estimates
```

```
# control_variates: Control variate values for each simulation

# control_variate_mean: Known mean of the control variate

covariance = np.cov(mc_estimates, control_variates)[0, 1]

variance = np.var(control_variates)

adjustment = covariance / variance * (control_variate_mean -
np.mean(control_variates))

adjusted_estimate = np.mean(mc_estimates) + adjustment

return adjusted_estimate

` ` `
```

Both antithetic variates and control variates stand as pillars in the quest for efficient stochastic simulation, each complementing the other in mitigating the variance inherent to Monte Carlo methods. By embedding these techniques within the Python ecosystem, financial analysts and quants can unveil the stochastic intricacies of option pricing with heightened precision, paving the way for more informed, robust trading strategies in the volatile arenas of financial markets.

Model Calibration with Python

Calibration involves adjusting the model parameters until the model's output aligns with market prices or historical data. This process is pivotal for stochastic volatility models like the Heston model, where parameters such as long-term volatility, mean reversion rate, and volatility of volatility are not directly observable and must be inferred from market prices of instruments like options.

The challenge lies in the multidimensional nature of the problem. Stochastic volatility models are often non-linear with respect to their parameters, making the calibration process inherently complex. Moreover, the calibration must be robust, ensuring that the model performs well not just on the data it was calibrated on but also on unseen data, to avoid overfitting.

Before calibration can begin, market data, typically option prices for various strikes and maturities, must be collected and prepared. This data serves as the target for the calibration process.

```python
import pandas as pd

# Load option data

option_data = pd.read_csv('option_prices.csv')

option_data['Mid'] = (option_data['Bid'] + option_data['Ask']) / 2
```

The objective function quantifies the difference between the model's predictions and the actual market data. A common choice is the sum of squared errors between model-implied volatilities and market-observed volatilities.

```python
from scipy.stats import norm

import numpy as np

def objective_function(params, market_prices, strikes, maturities):

model_prices = np.array([model_price(param, strike, maturity) for strike, maturity in zip(strikes, maturities)])

return np.sum((model_prices - market_prices) 2)
```

Utilizing SciPy's optimization libraries, we can search for the parameter set that minimizes the objective function. Gradient-based methods or global optimizers like differential evolution can be employed depending on the complexity of the model.

```python
from scipy.optimize import minimize
```

```
initial_guess = [ , , ] # Example initial guess


bounds = [(0, 1), (0, 1), (0, 1), (0, 1)]  # Example parameter
bounds


result   =   minimize(objective_function,   initial_guess,
args=(market_prices, strikes, maturities), bounds=bounds)


optimized_params = result.x


` ` `
```

After calibration, it's crucial to evaluate the model's performance on both the calibration data set and unseen data to check for overfitting. Techniques like cross-validation can be applied to assess the model's predictive power.

Model calibration with Python offers a flexible and powerful approach to aligning stochastic volatility models with market realities. Through the use of Python's extensive libraries and optimization routines, quants can achieve a level of precision and reliability in their models that is vital for developing robust trading strategies. The calibrated models serve as a cornerstone for pricing, risk management, and strategic decision-making in quantitative finance, showcasing Python's pivotal role in bridging theoretical models with practical market applications.

Preparing Market Data for Calibration Processes

Data preparation is a critical phase where raw market

data is cleaned, standardized, and transformed. This process enhances the quality and reliability of the data, which, in turn, impacts the precision of the calibration and the performance of the model. In the context of stochastic volatility models, the focus is primarily on option market data, given their sensitivity to volatility dynamics.

The first step involves gathering the necessary market data. For stochastic volatility model calibration, option chains for various financial instruments are essential. This data can be obtained from financial market databases, exchanges, or third-party data providers.

```python

import yfinance as yf

# Example: Fetching Apple's option chain

ticker = yf.Ticker("AAPL")

options_data = ticker.option_chain('next_expiry_date')

```

Raw market data often comes with its set of challenges - missing values, outliers, and errors that can skew the calibration process. Cleaning this data involves identifying and rectifying these issues, ensuring a dataset that accurately reflects market conditions.

```python

# Dropping rows with missing values

cleaned_data = options_data.dropna()

# Removing outliers based on option prices

q_low = cleaned_data['lastPrice'].quantile(0.01)

q_hi  = cleaned_data['lastPrice'].quantile(9)

filtered_data = cleaned_data[(cleaned_data['lastPrice'] < q_hi)
& (cleaned_data['lastPrice'] > q_low)]

```


Standardization of data refers to the process of bringing different datasets to a common format or scale. This is particularly important when combining data from multiple sources or when the data spans various instruments with differing units or scales.

```python

from sklearn.preprocessing import StandardScaler

# Example: Standardizing the 'strike' column
```

```python
scaler = StandardScaler()

filtered_data['strike_standardized']                         =
scaler.fit_transform(filtered_data[['strike']])
```

` ` `

Not all data points collected will be relevant for model calibration. Feature selection involves identifying the most relevant variables that influence the model's outcome. For volatility models, variables such as strike price, expiry, implied volatility, and bid-ask spreads are often key features.

` ` `python

Selecting relevant features for calibration

```python
features    =    filtered_data[['strike_standardized',    'expiry',
'impliedVolatility', 'bid', 'ask']]
```

` ` `

The final step involves transforming the selected features into a form that is directly usable in calibration algorithms. This can include computing the mid-price of options, converting dates to time-to-expiry in numerical format, and other model-specific transformations.

` ` `python

```
# Calculating the mid-price of options

features['mid_price'] = (features['bid'] + features['ask']) / 2

# Converting expiry dates to time-to-expiry

features['time_to_expiry'] = (pd.to_datetime(features['expiry'])
- pd.Timestamp.today()).dt.days

` ` `
```

The preparation of market data is a foundational step in the calibration process of stochastic volatility models. It ensures that the data fed into the calibration algorithms is of high quality, relevant, and structured in a way that aligns with the assumptions and requirements of the model. By meticulously executing these preparation steps, quants set the stage for a more accurate and reliable model calibration, enabling the development of robust trading strategies and risk management tools.

Implementing Optimization Routines to Fit Models to Market Data

Model calibration involves finding the set of model parameters that minimize the difference between market prices and model prices. This discrepancy is often measured using an objective function, such as the sum of squared errors (SSE) between the market observed option prices and the theoretical prices generated by the model.

Optimization algorithms are model calibration. These algorithms search for the parameter set that minimizes the objective function. Commonly used algorithms in model calibration include:

- Gradient Descent: A first-order iterative optimization algorithm for finding a local minimum of a differentiable function.

- Levenberg-Marquardt: An algorithm that interpolates between the Gauss-Newton algorithm and gradient descent.

- Genetic Algorithms: A heuristic search that mimics the process of natural selection to generate high-quality solutions to optimization problems.

For illustrating the calibration process, we'll focus on the Levenberg-Marquardt algorithm due to its effectiveness in dealing with complex, non-linear optimization problems common in financial modeling.

To implement the Levenberg-Marquardt algorithm for model calibration, we'll use the `scipy.optimize` module, which offers a suite of optimization algorithms. Our goal is to calibrate the Heston model to market data, adjusting its parameters to minimize the SSE between market and model prices.

```python

import numpy as np
```

```
from scipy.optimize import least_squares

# Objective function: Sum of squared errors between market
and model prices

def objective_function(params, market_prices, strikes,
maturities):

    # Extract Heston model parameters from params

    kappa, theta, sigma, rho, v0 = params

    # Calculate model prices using the Heston model (function not
    shown for brevity)

    model_prices = heston_model_prices(kappa, theta, sigma, rho,
    v0, strikes, maturities)

    # Compute the sum of squared errors

    return np.sum((market_prices - model_prices)2)

# Market data

market_prices = np.array([...]) # Market prices of options

strikes = np.array([...])      # Strike prices

maturities = np.array([...])    # Maturities
```

```
# Initial parameter guess

initial_guess = [, 0.04, -, 0.05]

# Run the Levenberg-Marquardt algorithm

result  =  least_squares(objective_function,  initial_guess,
args=(market_prices, strikes, maturities))

# Extract optimized parameters

optimized_params = result.x

` ` `
```

Upon completion of the optimization routine, it's crucial to analyze the results critically. This involves:

- Assessing the convergence of the algorithm: Ensuring that the algorithm has successfully converged to a solution.

- Evaluating the goodness-of-fit: Comparing the calibrated model prices with the market prices to assess the accuracy of the calibration.

- Sensitivity analysis: Analyzing how sensitive the calibrated parameters are to changes in the market data, which can provide insights into the model's robustness.

Assessing Calibration Quality: Goodness-of-Fit and Overfitting

Goodness-of-fit refers to the measure of how well a statistical model fits a set of observations. In the context of model calibration, it quantifies the closeness between the market prices and the prices predicted by the model. A variety of metrics can be employed to assess this fit:

- Root Mean Square Error (RMSE): Provides a measure of the differences between values predicted by a model and the values observed.

- R-squared (R^2): Indicates the percentage of the variance in the dependent variable that is predictable from the independent variable(s).

- AIC (Akaike Information Criterion) and BIC (Bayesian Information Criterion): These criteria not only account for the goodness-of-fit but also include a penalty term for the number of parameters in the model, thus discouraging overfitting.

Implementing these metrics in Python after model calibration can be straightforward, using libraries such as `numpy` for RMSE and `statsmodels` for AIC and BIC:

```python
import numpy as np

from statsmodels.tools.eval_measures import rmse, aic, bic
```

```
# Assuming market_prices and model_prices are numpy
arrays of the same shape

rmse_val = rmse(market_prices, model_prices)

print(f"RMSE: {rmse_val}")

# For AIC and BIC, assuming 'result' is the output from
optimization routine containing log-likelihood value

aic_val = aic(result.cost, len(market_prices), result.x.size)

bic_val = bic(result.cost, len(market_prices), result.x.size)

print(f"AIC: {aic_val}, BIC: {bic_val}")

```
```

While achieving a high goodness-of-fit is desirable, it is crucial to remain cautious of overfitting - a scenario where the model captures noise rather than the underlying process. Overfitting compromises the model's predictive power on new, unseen data. To combat overfitting, the following strategies are advisable:

- Cross-Validation: Splitting the data into training and validation sets, or employing more sophisticated techniques like K-fold cross-validation, helps in assessing how the model will generalize to an independent dataset.
```

- Regularization: Techniques such as Lasso (L1 regularization) and Ridge (L2 regularization) can be applied during the optimization process to introduce a penalty on the size of the coefficients, thus preventing the model from becoming overly complex.

- Simplicity: Sometimes, the simplest model that adequately explains the data is more desirable than a complex model with slightly better fit but higher risk of overfitting.

Here's an example of implementing cross-validation in Python:

```python

from sklearn.model_selection import cross_val_score

from sklearn.linear_model import Ridge

# Assuming 'X' is a feature matrix and 'y' are the observed market prices

model = Ridge(alpha=1.0)  # Example of regularization with Ridge regression

scores = cross_val_score(model, X, y, cv=5, scoring='neg_mean_squared_error')

print(f"Cross-Validation MSE scores: {-scores}")
```

` ` `

CHAPTER 6: ADVANCED TRADING STRATEGIES USING PYTHON

Algorithmic trading, utilizes algorithms to execute trades based on predefined criteria, without the need for human intervention. These criteria range from timing, price, and volume to more complex mathematical models. The evolution of algorithmic trading has been propelled by advances in computing power, enabling traders to implement strategies that can analyze vast amounts of data in real-time, identify market trends, and execute orders at a speed unattainable by humans.

The bedrock of any algorithmic trading strategy is its underlying model. A model's purpose is to predict future market movements based on historical data. Crucial to this endeavor is the application of stochastic volatility models which attempt to forecast the unpredictable movements of market prices and their volatility. The inclusion of stochastic elements in these models offers a more realistic representation of financial markets, acknowledging the inherent randomness and market sentiment fluctuations.

Integrating stochastic volatility into algorithmic trading strategies enhances their predictive power significantly. Traditional models, which often assume constant volatility, fail to capture the dynamic nature of financial markets. In contrast, stochastic models, such as the Heston model or SABR model, allow volatility to vary, providing a more accurate depiction of market conditions.

The implementation process begins with the calibration of these models to historical market data, ensuring that the model parameters precisely reflect observed market behavior. This step is critical, as precise calibration directly influences the strategy's effectiveness in real-time trading environments.

With a calibrated model at hand, the next phase involves the formulation of the trading strategy. This step includes defining the entry and exit points, position sizing, and risk management measures. A key advantage of algorithmic trading is the ability to rigorously backtest strategies using historical data. Backtesting assesses the strategy's viability, offering insights into its potential profitability and risk exposure in various market conditions.

The transition from a backtested strategy to real-time trading is a pivotal moment. Real-time implementation requires a robust infrastructure capable of processing high-frequency data streams, executing trades with minimal latency, and monitoring for anomalies or shifts in market behavior that could impact the strategy's performance.

Risk management is an integral component, ensuring that the strategy adheres to predefined risk thresholds. This involves setting stop-loss orders, diversifying trading instruments, and continuously monitoring the strategy's performance against market movements.

Algorithmic trading strategies are not without their challenges. Market conditions evolve, and strategies that once yielded high returns may become less effective. Continuous adaptation and refinement of the strategy, informed by ongoing market analysis and performance metrics, are essential for sustained success.

Moreover, the integration of machine learning techniques offers promising avenues for enhancing algorithmic strategies, enabling them to learn from new data, adapt to changing market dynamics, and uncover complex patterns previously unidentifiable.

Algorithmic trading strategies represent the pinnacle of trading's evolution, marrying the precision of mathematics with the insights of financial theory. The inclusion of stochastic volatility models marks a significant leap forward, offering a profound understanding of market movements. As we venture further into this domain, the boundaries of what's possible expand, driven by innovation, technology, and an unwavering pursuit of trading excellence.

Basics of Algorithmic Trading and Strategy Formulation

At its essence, algorithmic trading involves the use of computer algorithms to execute trades based on a set of criteria that can include price, timing, volume, and a myriad other market factors. This method of trading leverages computational algorithms to make trading decisions, execute trading orders, and manage risk, all at speeds and frequencies that are beyond human traders.

One of the primary advantages of algorithmic trading is its ability to process and analyze massive datasets rapidly, enabling the identification of profitable trading opportunities that would be impossible for a human trader to detect within the same timeframe. Moreover, it minimizes emotional decision-making, ensuring trading discipline is maintained even in highly volatile markets.

The development of a robust algorithmic trading strategy is grounded in several key pillars:

The foundation of any trading strategy lies in its underlying model and the quality of data it analyses. An exhaustive analysis of historical market data is critical to understanding market behavior and identifying patterns that can inform predictive models. The choice of model—whether it be based on simple moving averages, complex stochastic models, or machine learning algorithms—will dictate the strategy's approach to predicting market movements.

Designing an algorithmic trading strategy requires a clear definition of the objectives, including the expected return, risk tolerance, and time horizon of the investments. It involves specifying the criteria for trade entry and exit, order types, and any rules for money management and risk control. This stage also requires a decision on the frequency of trade—high-frequency trading, for instance, demands algorithms capable of making decisions in milliseconds.

A critical step in strategy formulation is backtesting, where the algorithm is tested against historical data to evaluate its performance. This process helps to uncover any potential issues with the strategy, such as overfitting, and allows for the fine-tuning of parameters. The objective is to ensure that the strategy can perform well across different market conditions.

Following backtesting, strategy optimization involves adjusting the model and its parameters to enhance performance. This may include altering the strategy's response to specific market indicators or optimizing order execution to minimize slippage and transaction costs.

An often-underestimated aspect of algorithmic trading is the importance of risk management. A well-formulated strategy must include robust risk management controls to protect against significant losses. This involves setting maximum loss thresholds, diversifying trades, and implementing stop-loss orders.

Formulating a successful algorithmic trading strategy is not without its challenges. Market conditions change, and a strategy that performs well in one market environment may falter in another. Additionally, transaction costs, slippage, and market impact can all erode profits. Therefore, continuous monitoring, testing, and refinement of the strategy are essential for long-term success.

Advancements in technology and computational power have greatly expanded the possibilities for algorithmic trading. The use of machine learning and artificial intelligence, for instance, offers new ways to model market behavior and predict price movements, providing a competitive edge in strategy development.

The formulation of an algorithmic trading strategy is both an art and a science, requiring a deep understanding of market dynamics, a solid foundation in quantitative analysis, and a meticulous approach to testing and optimization. As financial markets continue to evolve, so too will the strategies that navigate them, always seeking the optimal path through the complexity of market fluctuations.

Incorporating Stochastic Volatility Models into Trading Algorithms

Stochastic volatility models are at the forefront of financial mathematics, offering a more nuanced representation of market volatility than traditional models. Unlike constant volatility models, which assume a static volatility parameter, stochastic volatility models recognize that market volatility is dynamic, influenced by a myriad of factors, and subject to change over time. This dynamism mirrors the true nature of financial markets, where volatility exhibits unpredictable fluctuations, affecting asset prices and trading opportunities.

The integration of stochastic volatility models into trading algorithms enables traders and quantitative analysts to capture this volatility dynamic, leading to more accurate market predictions and potentially higher returns. Models such as the Heston model or the SABR model allow for a probabilistic approach to volatility, incorporating random fluctuations and providing a more realistic framework for option pricing and risk management.

The technical process of incorporating stochastic volatility models into trading algorithms involves several key steps:

1. Model Selection: Choosing the appropriate stochastic volatility model is paramount. The model must align with the specific market being traded, the asset class, and the desired trading frequency. The Heston model, for example, is popular for its analytical tractability and ability to model mean reversion in volatility, making it suitable for equity markets.

2. Parameter Estimation: Once a model is selected, estimating its parameters accurately is crucial. This often involves sophisticated statistical techniques and the analysis of historical market data. The accuracy of these parameters directly impacts the predictive power of the trading algorithm.

3. Simulation and Backtesting: Incorporating the model into the trading algorithm requires rigorous backtesting. By simulating the algorithm's performance using historical data, traders can assess how well the stochastic volatility model enhances the algorithm's predictive accuracy and profitability. This step is critical for fine-tuning the model and algorithm parameters.

4. Execution and Risk Management: With the model integrated and backtested, the algorithm can then be deployed in live trading. However, effective execution and risk management strategies must be in place to navigate the inherent uncertainties of using stochastic models. This includes setting appropriate stop-loss orders, managing position sizes, and continuously monitoring model performance.

Incorporating stochastic volatility models into trading algorithms offers several benefits, including improved accuracy in predicting price movements, enhanced risk management capabilities, and the potential for higher returns.

These models provide a more nuanced understanding of market dynamics, allowing algorithms to adjust trading strategies dynamically as market conditions change.

However, the integration of these models also presents challenges. The complexity of stochastic volatility models requires a deep understanding of financial mathematics and computational methods. Parameter estimation and model calibration can be computationally intensive, requiring advanced techniques and significant processing power. Moreover, the models' predictive accuracy can be influenced by sudden market shocks or events that defy historical patterns.

The journey of incorporating stochastic volatility models into trading algorithms is one of continuous learning and adaptation. As financial markets evolve and new data becomes available, these models must be periodically re-evaluated and refined. The intersection of financial theory, computational power, and real-world trading experience is where successful algorithmic trading strategies are forged. With the right approach, stochastic volatility models offer a powerful tool for navigating the complexities of the financial markets, providing traders with a competitive edge in their algorithmic strategies.

Backtesting Strategies with Historical Data

Historical market data forms the backbone of the backtesting process. This data encompasses a wide array of market indicators, including but not limited to, asset prices, trading volumes, bid-ask spreads, and implied volatility levels. The depth and quality of this data directly influence the reliability of backtesting results. For strategies that leverage stochastic volatility models, accessing granular historical volatility data is crucial for accurately simulating how these models would have performed in varying market conditions.

The process of backtesting an algorithmic trading strategy can be broken down into several critical steps:

1. Data Preparation: This involves collecting, cleaning, and preparing historical market data for analysis. The data must be free from biases and anomalies that could distort backtesting results. For strategies utilizing stochastic volatility models, the accuracy and granularity of volatility data are paramount.

2. Strategy Definition: Clearly defining the trading strategy and its rules is essential before backtesting can commence. This includes specifying the conditions under which trades will be initiated, managed, and closed. For strategies based on stochastic volatility, this might involve setting thresholds for entering or exiting trades based on volatility levels predicted by the model.

3. Simulation: The trading strategy is then simulated on historical data, with the algorithm making hypothetical trades according to its predefined rules. This step often requires sophisticated software capable of processing vast datasets and simulating trades with high accuracy.

4. Performance Assessment: After the simulation, the performance of the trading strategy is evaluated using various metrics such as return on investment (ROI), Sharpe ratio, maximum drawdown, and win-loss ratio. This assessment provides insights into the strategy's profitability, risk, and robustness across different market conditions.

5. Optimization: Based on the performance assessment, the trading strategy and its underlying model parameters can be adjusted and optimized to improve results. This may involve tweaking entry/exit criteria, risk management rules, or parameters of the stochastic volatility model itself.

6. Validation: Finally, the optimized strategy is validated by backtesting it on a different set of historical data or out-of-sample data. This step helps verify the strategy's effectiveness and guards against overfitting to the initial dataset.

While backtesting is an invaluable tool in strategy development, it is not without its challenges. One of the key issues is the risk of overfitting, where a strategy is overly optimized to past data and fails to perform in future conditions. Additionally, historical data, no matter how comprehensive, can never fully capture the complexity and unpredictability of future market movements. Strategies based on stochastic volatility models must also contend with the models' inherent assumptions and limitations.

Moreover, transaction costs, market impact, and liquidity constraints are often underrepresented in backtesting scenarios, which can lead to overly optimistic estimates of strategy performance. It is crucial for quants and traders to remain mindful of these factors and apply conservative assumptions where necessary.

Backtesting strategies with historical data is an yet essential process in the development of algorithmic trading strategies. It provides a framework for evaluating the efficacy of strategies underpinned by stochastic volatility models, enabling traders to refine and optimize their approaches based on empirical evidence. However, the process also demands a critical understanding of its limitations and challenges, underscoring the importance of a balanced and informed approach to strategy development and risk management.

Risk Management Techniques

Before diving deep into risk management techniques, it is imperative to acknowledge the multifaceted nature of market risks. Price volatility, liquidity fluctuations, and geopolitical events are but a few factors that can precipitate rapid changes in market conditions. Stochastic volatility models, by their nature, attempt to capture the essence of market volatility; however, their integration into risk management strategies demands a nuanced understanding of their predictive capabilities and limitations.

The application of stochastic volatility models in risk management is predicated on their ability to provide probabilistic forecasts of volatility. These forecasts serve as critical inputs in the construction of risk measures such as Value at Risk (VaR) and Conditional Value at Risk (CVaR), which estimate potential losses over specified time horizons and confidence levels. By incorporating stochastic volatility into these calculations, traders and risk managers can gain a more dynamic and nuanced view of risk exposure across different market scenarios.

Value at Risk has established itself as a cornerstone metric in financial risk management. It offers a quantifiable estimate of the maximum expected loss over a given time frame, under normal market conditions, and within a defined confidence interval. Implementing VaR within the context of stochastic volatility involves simulating a vast array of price paths for assets, utilizing the probabilistic outcomes generated by the volatility models. This simulation process, often conducted through Monte Carlo methods, enables the estimation of loss distributions from which the VaR can be derived.

While VaR provides insights into potential losses, it does not account for the severity of losses that might occur beyond the VaR threshold. This is where Conditional Value at Risk (CVaR), also known as Expected Shortfall, comes into play. CVaR delves deeper, offering an average of the losses that exceed the VaR, thus providing a more comprehensive view of the tail risk. The integration of stochastic volatility models into CVaR calculations enhances the accuracy of these estimates, particularly in capturing the tail behavior of asset price distributions.

Beyond the probabilistic confines of VaR and CVaR, stress testing and scenario analysis offer avenues to explore the impacts of extreme market events. These techniques involve applying hypothetical or historical adverse market scenarios to evaluate the resilience of trading strategies and portfolios. Stochastic volatility models contribute by enabling the simulation of extreme volatility conditions, thus enriching the stress testing process with detailed insights into how trading strategies might perform under such duress.

mitigating market risk lies the principle of diversification. Portfolio optimization techniques, grounded in modern portfolio theory, strive to balance the trade-off between risk and return. Stochastic volatility models enhance this process by providing dynamic estimates of volatility and correlations, which are pivotal in constructing diversified portfolios that can withstand volatility shifts. By optimizing asset allocation based on stochastic volatility forecasts, traders can achieve more efficient risk-adjusted returns.

While stochastic volatility models and the associated risk management techniques offer profound insights, they are not without limitations. The accuracy of these models is contingent upon the quality of the data and the appropriateness of the model assumptions to real-world dynamics. Furthermore, the ethical use of these models necessitates transparency, especially in communicating the associated risks and uncertainties to stakeholders.

The dance between stochastic volatility models and risk management techniques is a testament to the sophistication of modern quantitative finance. By judiciously applying these models within comprehensive risk management frameworks, traders and analysts can navigate the uncertainties of the financial markets with greater confidence and foresight. Yet, the journey does not end here; continuous innovation and ethical vigilance remain paramount in advancing the frontier of risk management strategies.

Quantitative Risk Management Basics

quantitative risk management operates within a structured framework that encompasses risk identification, measurement, assessment, and mitigation. This framework is vital for understanding the multifarious nature of financial risks, including market risk, credit risk, operational risk, and liquidity risk. Each of these risk types demands a tailored approach, leveraging specific models and metrics to quantify and analyze risk exposure accurately.

The initial stage in the risk management process involves

identifying potential risks that could negatively impact financial objectives. This step is followed by the measurement of risk, which is where quantitative methods come into play. Techniques such as historical simulation, variance-covariance analysis, and extreme value theory are employed to measure the magnitude and probability of risk factors. These measurements are crucial for constructing a comprehensive risk profile that informs subsequent management strategies.

With a quantified risk profile at hand, the next step involves the assessment of how these risks interact with the financial institution's tolerance levels and objectives. This assessment guides the selection of appropriate risk mitigation strategies, which may include hedging, diversification, insurance, or risk transfer. Quantitative models, such as those based on stochastic volatility, play a pivotal role in designing these strategies, enabling the optimization of risk-return trade-offs.

As previously introduced, Value at Risk (VaR) remains a cornerstone metric in risk measurement, providing a clear, quantifiable estimate of potential losses. Quantitative risk management expands on basic VaR models to include variants such as Historical VaR, Parametric VaR, and Monte Carlo VaR, each offering distinct advantages in different contexts. Moreover, techniques such as backtesting VaR and stress testing are employed to validate the models and ensure their reliability under varied market conditions.

Recognizing the limitations of VaR, quantitative risk management also embraces more sophisticated metrics like Conditional Value at Risk (CVaR), liquidity-adjusted VaR, and incremental risk charge. These metrics offer deeper insights into tail risks, liquidity considerations, and the marginal impact of individual assets on portfolio risk. The use of stochastic models, including those that account for changes in volatility and correlation, enriches the analysis, providing a dynamic and nuanced view of risk exposures.

The evolution of quantitative risk management is closely intertwined with advancements in technology and the proliferation of big data. High-performance computing enables the processing of vast datasets, allowing for more accurate and granular risk analyses. Machine learning and artificial intelligence further augment traditional models, introducing capabilities for pattern recognition, anomaly detection, and predictive analytics. These technological tools are instrumental in enhancing the precision and agility of risk management practices.

An integral component of quantitative risk management is the acknowledgment of model risk—the risk of losses resulting from the use of inadequate or incorrect models. This awareness underscores the importance of model validation, governance, and ethical considerations in model development and application. Transparency, integrity, and continuous improvement are vital for mitigating model risk and fostering trust among stakeholders.

Quantitative risk management embodies a rigorous and methodical approach to navigating the complexities of financial markets. By grounding risk management practices in mathematical and statistical models, financial institutions can better anticipate, understand, and mitigate risks. As the financial landscape continues to evolve, so too will the methodologies and technologies at the disposal of quantitative risk managers, perpetually enhancing the robustness and resilience of financial systems against the backdrop of uncertainty.

Portfolio Optimization and Value-at-Risk (VaR) Calculations Using Stochastic Models

Portfolio optimization is the process of selecting the best portfolio (asset distribution) out of the set of all portfolios being considered, according to some objective. The objective typically maximizes factors such as expected return, and minimizes costs like financial risk. Stochastic models, by incorporating random variables, enable a more nuanced understanding of market volatility and asset price movements. This dynamic approach allows investors to simulate various market scenarios and their potential impacts on portfolio performance.

The foundation of portfolio optimization rests on Harry Markowitz's Modern Portfolio Theory (MPT), which emphasizes the balance between risk and return. MPT, however, assumes a constant volatility, a limitation that stochastic models overcome by acknowledging volatility's unpredictable nature. By integrating stochastic volatility into MPT, investors can adjust their portfolios in anticipation of possible market changes, rather than reacting post-factum.

Value-at-Risk (VaR) is a widely used risk measure that estimates the maximum potential loss of a portfolio over a given time period at a specific confidence level, under normal market conditions. The integration of stochastic models into VaR calculations introduces a dynamic aspect to risk measurement, accounting for volatility swings and abrupt market shifts. This results in a more comprehensive and realistic measure of potential losses.

The calculation of VaR utilizing stochastic volatility models involves simulating a wide range of market conditions and their effects on portfolio value. Techniques such as the Monte Carlo simulation are particularly effective, as they generate numerous potential future asset prices by random sampling from the probability distributions of market risks. This method provides a distribution of possible outcomes from which VaR can be derived.

Optimizing a portfolio in the context of stochastic volatility involves identifying the optimal asset allocation that minimizes risk for a given level of expected return, or alternatively, maximizes return for a given level of risk. The process requires solving complex optimization problems that consider the stochastic nature of asset returns and volatilities. This can be achieved through numerical methods and optimization algorithms that search for the optimal portfolio composition.

Monte Carlo simulations play a crucial role in portfolio optimization under stochastic volatility. By simulating thousands of potential future states of the market, Monte Carlo methods enable the evaluation of portfolio performance across a vast spectrum of scenarios. This data-driven approach informs decision-making regarding asset allocation, weighting, and hedging strategies, facilitating the construction of portfolios that are robust across various market conditions.

While the integration of stochastic models into portfolio optimization and VaR calculations offers a more dynamic and informed approach to risk management, it is not without challenges. The complexity of these models requires sophisticated computational resources and deep expertise in quantitative finance. Additionally, the reliability of the models is contingent upon the accuracy of the input data and the assumptions made about market behavior.

Moreover, ethical considerations concerning transparency and the potential for model risk necessitate rigorous validation and governance processes. As with all models, there is a danger of over-reliance on quantitative methods, underscoring the importance of maintaining a balance between model-driven insights and fundamental analysis.

The fusion of stochastic models with portfolio optimization and VaR calculations represents a formidable advancement in quantitative finance. By embracing the inherent uncertainty of financial markets, these models equip investors with the tools to navigate volatility, enhance portfolio resilience, and optimize risk-return profiles. As the financial landscape evolves, the ongoing development and refinement of stochastic approaches will continue to play a pivotal role in shaping effective investment strategies.

Applying Machine Learning for Improved Risk Assessment

Machine learning, is about teaching computers to learn from and make decisions based on data. In the context of risk management, this capability translates into analyzing historical financial data to identify patterns, trends, and correlations that might not be apparent to human analysts. ML algorithms, ranging from supervised learning models like regression and classification to unsupervised learning models like clustering and dimensionality reduction, offer diverse tools for dissecting financial data.

One of the most compelling applications of ML in risk

assessment is predictive analytics. ML models can process vast amounts of historical data to forecast future market movements, volatility spikes, and potential risk scenarios. These forecasts enable risk managers to anticipate and mitigate risks before they materialize, shifting the paradigm from reactive to proactive risk management.

Credit risk evaluation is a prime area where ML has made significant inroads. Traditional credit scoring models often rely on a narrow set of financial indicators and borrower characteristics. In contrast, ML models can incorporate a broader array of data points, including non-traditional and unstructured data such as transaction histories, social media activity, and even geographical information. By doing so, ML models can offer more accurate and individualized credit risk assessments.

ML algorithms also play a crucial role in managing market and operational risks. For market risk, ML models can analyze complex market dynamics and the interplay between different financial instruments to predict volatility and market downturns. For operational risk, ML can help identify patterns indicative of fraud, compliance breaches, or system failures, thereby enhancing the resilience of financial operations.

The efficacy of ML models is heavily dependent on the quality and granularity of the available data. Incomplete, outdated, or biased data sets can lead to inaccurate risk assessments, potentially exacerbating rather than mitigating risk. Ensuring data integrity and addressing privacy concerns are paramount for the successful application of ML in risk assessment.

ML models, especially deep learning networks, can be highly complex, making them difficult to interpret even for experts.

This "black box" nature poses challenges for risk management, where understanding the rationale behind risk assessments is crucial for decision-making and compliance. Efforts to develop more interpretable ML models and techniques for explaining model decisions are ongoing areas of research.

Integrating ML into existing risk management frameworks presents operational challenges. It requires not only technical integration but also a cultural shift within organizations towards data-driven decision-making. Training and development, along with cross-functional collaboration, are essential to harness the full potential of ML in risk assessment.

Applying machine learning to risk assessment represents a paradigm shift in how financial risks are analyzed, predicted, and managed. With its ability to process and learn from vast datasets, ML offers unparalleled insights into risk factors and dynamics, enabling more informed and proactive risk management strategies. However, realizing this potential requires overcoming significant challenges, including data quality, model interpretability, and integration into existing risk frameworks. As the field of quantitative finance continues to evolve, the role of machine learning in shaping the future of risk assessment will undoubtedly expand, promising more sophisticated and effective risk management solutions.

Real-time Data and High-frequency Trading

high-frequency trading lies the indispensable asset of real-time data. This data, characterized by its instantaneous nature, includes price movements, trading volumes, and order book dynamics, providing a granular view of market conditions as they unfold. The ability to access and process this data in real-time is what distinguishes high-frequency traders from traditional market participants.

The exploitation of real-time data in HFT is made possible through cutting-edge technological infrastructure. High-speed data feeds, ultra-low latency networks, and advanced computing hardware form the backbone of HFT operations, enabling traders to receive, analyze, and act upon market information in milliseconds. This technological prowess is complemented by sophisticated algorithms capable of parsing vast streams of data to identify profitable trading signals.

High-frequency trading algorithms are engineered with complexity and adaptability to thrive in the fast-paced market environment. They incorporate a variety of analytical techniques, including statistical arbitrage, market making, and event-driven strategies, all designed to capitalize on minute price discrepancies and patterns that emerge within fractions of a second.

The integration of machine learning into HFT algorithms marks a significant evolution in how real-time data is utilized. These models, trained on historical and real-time market data, predict price movements and identify optimal entry and exit points for trades. Machine learning algorithms continually adapt to changing market dynamics, enhancing their predictive accuracy and the effectiveness of trading strategies.

While high-frequency trading offers substantial profit potential, it also introduces challenges such as market impact and systemic risk. The sheer volume of trades executed by HFT algorithms can lead to significant price movements, affecting liquidity and volatility. Additionally, the interconnectedness of HFT strategies can amplify market shocks, posing challenges to market stability.

high-frequency trading is also subject to regulatory scrutiny and ethical considerations. Regulators aim to ensure that HFT practices contribute to healthy market functioning without disadvantaging other market participants. Ethical debates surround the fairness of HFT, given its reliance on technological superiority and access to real-time data.

The future of real-time data and high-frequency trading is likely to witness further advancements in data analytics and artificial intelligence. As computational capabilities continue to evolve, the potential for developing more sophisticated algorithms that can interpret complex market signals in real-time will expand. This progression promises to further refine the speed and accuracy of HFT strategies.

High-frequency traders must remain agile, adapting to the changing market landscape, regulatory updates, and technological advancements. The ongoing innovation in financial technology and data science will shape the strategies and tools at the disposal of HFT practitioners, requiring continuous learning and adaptation.

Real-time data and high-frequency trading stand at the confluence of technology and finance, driving forward the capabilities of market participants to engage with financial markets at unparalleled speeds. Through the intelligent application of real-time data analytics, machine learning, and sophisticated algorithmic strategies, HFT continues to push the boundaries of what is possible in trading. However, navigating this landscape requires careful consideration of the associated challenges, regulatory frameworks, and the impact on market integrity. As the domain of HFT evolves, so too will the strategies and technologies that underpin its success, heralding a new era of trading in the digital age.

Handling and Analysis of Real-Time Financial Data in Python

Python's prominence in financial data analysis can be attributed to its simplicity and the powerful libraries it supports. Libraries such as Pandas for data manipulation, NumPy for numerical analysis, and matplotlib for data visualization are foundational. However, handling real-time data introduces the need for more specialized libraries and tools.

Real-time financial data collection in Python is predominantly facilitated through APIs (Application Programming Interfaces) provided by data vendors and trading platforms. Libraries such as `requests` for HTTP requests and `websocket-client` for WebSocket connections are essential for accessing streaming data. The `pandas_datareader` library also offers convenient functions to fetch data from various sources, although its real-time capabilities depend on the data provider.

For instance, connecting to a WebSocket for live trade data could be achieved as follows:

```python

import websocket
```

```python
import json

def on_message(ws, message):

data = json.loads(message)

print("New data received:", data)

def on_error(ws, error):

print("Error:", error)

def on_close(ws):

print(" connection closed ")

def on_open(ws):

print("Connection opened")

if __name__ == "__main__":

ws              =              websocket.WebSocketApp("wss://
api.tradingplatform.com/socket/websocket",

on_open=on_open,

on_message=on_message,
```

on_error=on_error,

on_close=on_close)

ws.run_forever()

```
` ` `
```

This example demonstrates how to establish a WebSocket connection to a hypothetical trading platform, allowing for the reception of live trading data.

Upon collecting real-time financial data, the next immediate steps involve its processing and analysis. The key challenge here is the velocity and volume of the data, which necessitate efficient processing pipelines to extract actionable insights without significant latency.

The `pandas` library, renowned for its powerful data manipulation capabilities, can be employed to structure real-time data into DataFrame objects for real-time analysis. Operations such as filtering, aggregation, and computation of financial indicators become straightforward with pandas.

For real-time analysis, moving averages and other financial indicators are commonly calculated to inform trading decisions. Python's `ta-lib` library, a wrapper for the Technical Analysis Library, offers a broad set of functions for computing technical indicators over stock price data.

```python
```

```python
import pandas as pd

import numpy as np

import talib

# Assuming real-time data is being appended to
'real_time_data_df'

real_time_data_df['SMA'] =
talib.SMA(real_time_data_df['close'], timeperiod=20)

real_time_data_df['EMA'] =
talib.EMA(real_time_data_df['close'], timeperiod=20)

print(real_time_data_df.tail())
```

```

This snippet demonstrates the computation of Simple Moving Average (SMA) and Exponential Moving Average (EMA) on a DataFrame containing real-time closing prices.

Monitoring real-time trading data and indicators is crucial for timely decision-making. Python's `matplotlib` and `plotly` libraries offer dynamic plotting capabilities that can be integrated into dashboards for live data monitoring. `Dash` by Plotly, for instance, enables the creation of interactive, web-based dashboards that update in real-time as new data arrives.
```

Handling real-time financial data with Python is not devoid of challenges. Key considerations include managing data latency, ensuring the reliability of data streams, and handling exceptions gracefully. Moreover, computational efficiency becomes paramount as the volume of data and complexity of analysis increase.

Python's flexibility, coupled with its rich set of libraries, makes it an invaluable tool for handling and analyzing real-time financial data. As financial markets continue to evolve towards greater speed and complexity, the ability to process and analyze data in real-time will remain a critical advantage. Through continuous learning and adaptation, financial analysts and traders can harness the power of Python to navigate the fast-paced world of finance with confidence and precision.

Adapting Models for High-Frequency Trading Environments

High-frequency trading (HFT) has reshaped the landscape of financial markets, fueled by advancements in technology and sophisticated mathematical models. These trading strategies, executed by computers, are designed to move in and out of positions in fractions of a second. The transition toward HFT necessitates a reevaluation and adaptation of traditional stochastic volatility models to thrive in an environment where milliseconds can mean the difference between profit and loss.

The quintessential characteristic of high-frequency trading environments is their reliance on speed and precision. Stochastic volatility models, traditionally used for forecasting market movements over days or weeks, must be recalibrated for the microsecond trading horizon of HFT. This recalibration involves both the refinement of the models' mathematical framework and the optimization of their computational algorithms for faster execution.

In high-frequency trading, the computational efficiency of a model is paramount. Adapting stochastic volatility models for HFT involves simplifying complex equations without compromising their predictive power. Techniques such as dimensionality reduction, approximation algorithms, and parallel computing are pivotal in achieving this goal.

For instance, leveraging Python's multiprocessing library can facilitate the parallel execution of Monte Carlo simulations, a common technique in stochastic model calibration:

```python

from multiprocessing import Pool

import numpy as np

def monte_carlo_simulation(params):

# Placeholder for a complex calculation

np.random.seed(params)

return np.random.normal(0, 1, 100).mean()

if __name__ == '__main__':
```

```
pool = Pool(processes=4)  # Number of concurrent processes

params = [1, 2, 3, 4]  # Example parameters for different
simulations

results = pool.map(monte_carlo_simulation, params)

print(results)

` ` `
```

This example demonstrates how parallel processing can be utilized to expedite computationally intensive tasks inherent in stochastic volatility models.

High-frequency trading models thrive on real-time market data. The latency in data collection, processing, and execution is a critical factor that influences the success of HFT strategies. Python libraries such as `asyncio` for asynchronous programming can be instrumental in managing real-time data feeds efficiently, ensuring that the models operate with the minimal time lag possible.

Adapting models for HFT also involves incorporating mechanisms to dynamically adjust to market conditions. This might include real-time calibration of model parameters based on incoming data streams or the integration of machine learning algorithms to predict parameter shifts before they occur.

Risk management takes on a new dimension in high-frequency trading environments. The traditional stochastic volatility models must be enhanced to account for unique HFT risks such as market impact, liquidity risk, and the potential for systemic errors in automated execution systems.

Incorporating sophisticated risk management algorithms directly into the trading model can help mitigate these risks. For example, dynamic stop-loss mechanisms can be programmed to automatically liquidate positions if certain risk thresholds are breached.

The adaptation of stochastic models for HFT must also consider regulatory and ethical implications. As regulators worldwide scrutinize high-frequency trading practices, models must be designed with transparency and compliance in mind. This includes the capability to provide detailed reporting on trading activities and to ensure that trading strategies do not contribute to market disruption.

Adapting stochastic volatility models for high-frequency trading environments is a complex but essential endeavor as financial markets evolve. Through enhanced computational efficiency, real-time data processing, sophisticated risk management, and adherence to regulatory standards, these models can be finely tuned to capture the opportunities presented by the fast-paced world of HFT. Python, with its rich ecosystem of libraries and its capability for rapid prototyping and execution, remains a cornerstone technology in this adaptation process. As the financial industry continues to innovate, the agility to adapt to changing market dynamics will be critical for sustained success in high-frequency trading.

Challenges and Solutions for Latency and Computational

Efficiency

Latency can be introduced at multiple points in the trading process, including data acquisition, analysis, decision-making, and execution. One common source is the physical distance between the trader's servers and the exchange's data centers. Another is the inefficiency in data processing pipelines, where the computational load can delay the analysis and execution of trades.

Proximity Hosting: One effective solution is proximity hosting, which involves placing trading servers geographically close to an exchange's data center to minimize travel time for data, thereby reducing latency.

Streamlining Data Processing: Optimizing the codebase for efficiency can significantly reduce processing times. Python offers numerous opportunities for such optimization, including the use of efficient data structures and algorithms. For instance, employing pandas' DataFrame operations can expedite data manipulations, while NumPy can handle numerical calculations more swiftly than pure Python code.

```python
import pandas as pd

import numpy as np

# Optimizing data processing with pandas and NumPy

data    =    pd.DataFrame(np.random.randn(1000,    4),
```

columns=list('ABCD'))

optimized_result = data.apply(np.sum) # Using NumPy's sum operation for efficiency

` ` `

The complexity of models used in HFT can lead to computational bottlenecks, especially when dealing with large datasets or executing multiple models in parallel.

One approach to overcoming these bottlenecks is through parallel computing, where tasks are distributed across multiple processing units. Python's `concurrent.futures` module is a powerful tool for implementing parallel execution:

` ` `python

from concurrent.futures import ThreadPoolExecutor

import numpy as np

def compute_model(inputs):

Placeholder for a computationally intensive model

return np.mean(inputs)

Example: Parallel execution of a computational model

```
with ThreadPoolExecutor(max_workers=4) as executor:

futures        =        [executor.submit(compute_model,
np.random.rand(1000)) for _ in range(4)]

results = [f.result() for f in futures]

` ` `
```

Efficient data handling and storage can also play a significant role in enhancing computational efficiency. Techniques such as data compression and chunking can reduce the memory footprint and improve the speed of data-intensive operations.

Adaptive algorithms can dynamically adjust their complexity based on the current market conditions and the available computational resources. This approach allows for a balance between the accuracy of the models and the computational resources they consume, optimizing for both performance and efficiency.

While optimizing for latency and computational efficiency, it's crucial to maintain compliance with regulatory standards. This includes ensuring that the strategies do not introduce excessive volatility into the market or disadvantage other market participants.

Addressing the challenges of latency and computational efficiency in high-frequency trading is a multidimensional endeavor. It requires a nuanced understanding of the sources of delay and inefficiency, alongside a toolkit of technological and strategic solutions. Python, with its extensive libraries and support for parallel computing, offers a versatile platform for developing and executing high-performance trading strategies. By harnessing these technologies and approaches, traders can navigate the landscape of HFT, optimizing their operations for speed, efficiency, and regulatory compliance.

CHAPTER 7: ANALYZING HISTORICAL MARKET EVENTS

In the annals of financial history, few events have reshaped the landscape of global finance as profoundly as the 2008 financial crisis. This cataclysmic event, originating from the United States' financial sector, cascaded into a global economic downturn, the likes of which hadn't been seen since the Great Depression. Its repercussions on volatility, market dynamics, and the overarching structure of financial regulations have since become a focal point of study, particularly through the lens of stochastic volatility models.

The seeds of the crisis were sown in the fertile ground of housing market speculation, fertilized by an era of low interest rates and loose lending practices. Financial institutions, driven by an insatiable appetite for profit, devised complex mortgage-backed securities (MBS) and collateralized debt obligations (CDOs), whose value was intricately tied to the performance of the housing market. As housing prices soared, the bubble grew larger, inflated by speculative investments and an unwavering belief in the market's invincibility.

Stochastic volatility models, which are designed to capture the random nature of market volatility, play a critical role in understanding the dynamics of the crisis. As the housing market began to falter, the volatility in financial markets surged. Traditional models, which assumed constant volatility, were ill-equipped to handle the rapid fluctuations, leading to massive mispricings of risk and contributing to the systemic collapse of financial institutions.

Using stochastic volatility models like the Heston model, financial analysts can retrospectively simulate the market conditions leading up to the crisis, revealing how a more nuanced understanding of volatility could have potentially signaled the impending collapse. Furthermore, these models illustrate the dramatic increase in market volatility during the crisis, marked by sharp declines in stock prices and significant spikes in the VIX, often referred to as the "fear index."

The 2008 financial crisis underscored the limitations of traditional financial models and highlighted the importance of stochastic volatility models in capturing the complex dynamics of financial markets. These models, which account for the unpredictable and erratic behavior of volatility, became instrumental in dissecting the crisis's causes and effects. They provided insights into the market's panic-driven reactions and the cascading failures of financial institutions, offering valuable lessons for future risk management practices.

The aftermath of the crisis brought about a sweeping overhaul of financial regulations and a reevaluation of risk management strategies. Stochastic volatility models, with their ability to capture the multifaceted nature of market volatility, have since played a pivotal role in shaping the new regulatory landscape. They have informed the development of stress testing frameworks, improved the calibration of risk models, and enhanced the robustness of financial institutions against future shocks.

The 2008 financial crisis serves as a stark reminder of the complexities inherent in financial markets and the catastrophic consequences of overlooking these complexities. By integrating stochastic volatility models into financial analysis, the industry has taken significant strides toward a deeper, more nuanced understanding of market dynamics. These models stand at the forefront of ongoing efforts to fortify the financial system, ensuring that the lessons of the crisis continue to inform and guide the development of more resilient financial practices and regulations. Through the lens of stochastic volatility, the 2008 crisis not only offers a cautionary tale but also illuminates the path forward toward a more stable and secure financial future.

Overview of the 2008 Crisis and Its Impact on Volatility

The prelude to the crisis was characterized by an unprecedented expansion of credit and a housing boom, facilitated by low interest rates and an abundance of liquidity in the global financial system. Financial innovation led to the creation of complex derivative instruments, such as mortgage-backed securities (MBS) and collateralized debt obligations (CDOs), which were underpinned by subprime mortgages. These instruments were pivotal in distributing risk across the financial system but also obscured the true extent of credit exposure.

As default rates on subprime mortgages began to climb, the valuation of these securities plummeted, exposing financial institutions to massive losses. This set off a chain reaction, leading to a credit crunch that stifled economic activity worldwide. The collapse of Lehman Brothers in September 2008 marked the zenith of the crisis, sending shockwaves through the global financial system. Stock markets plunged, and volatility indices, such as the VIX, surged to record levels, reflecting unprecedented uncertainty and fear in the market.

The crisis underscored volatility's crucial role in financial markets. Prior to the crisis, volatility was largely viewed through the prism of historical models that assumed market movements followed a Gaussian distribution with predictable swings. However, the extreme events of 2008 demonstrated that volatility is inherently stochastic, exhibiting jumps and spikes that defy traditional modeling approaches.

The impact of the crisis on volatility was twofold. Firstly, it led to a paradigm shift in how volatility is conceptualized and modeled, with a greater emphasis on stochastic volatility models capable of capturing extreme market conditions. Secondly, it highlighted the need for robust risk management practices that account for fat-tail events and systemic risks.

In the aftermath of the crisis, stochastic volatility models gained prominence for their ability to more accurately capture the dynamics of financial markets in distress. The Heston model, for example, became a critical tool for options pricing and risk management, offering insights into the market's behavior under stress. These models allowed for a better understanding of the volatility smile—a market phenomenon that became particularly pronounced during the crisis—and the pricing of exotic options in turbulent markets.

The crisis catalyzed a reevaluation of market dynamics and

the factors driving volatility. It became evident that liquidity, or the lack thereof, played a significant role in exacerbating market movements. The interconnectivity of global financial markets meant that shocks in one part of the world could quickly propagate, leading to increased correlation among asset classes and heightened systemic risk.

The 2008 financial crisis was a defining moment that reshaped the landscape of financial markets and the theoretical frameworks used to understand them. It brought to the fore the critical importance of volatility, not just as a measure of market risk but as a fundamental characteristic of financial markets that requires sophisticated modeling and analysis. As we continue to navigate the complexities of global finance, the lessons learned from the crisis and the advancements in stochastic volatility modeling remain invaluable in guiding risk management decisions and financial regulation policies.

5 Analysis of Volatility Patterns Using Stochastic Models

Post-crisis, the financial academia and industry alike recognized the limitations of traditional volatility models that failed to predict or accommodate the extreme market behaviors observed during 2008. This acknowledgment spurred the development and adoption of enhanced stochastic models that could capture the erratic movements of markets more accurately. Among these, the Heston model, with its capability to model volatility as a stochastic process itself, gained significant traction. The model's ability to incorporate volatility smile dynamics—previously a challenging endeavor —enabled a more nuanced understanding of market sentiment and pricing anomalies.

The application of stochastic volatility models extended

beyond academic curiosity, proving instrumental in the recalibration of risk management frameworks. Financial institutions, learning from the painful lessons of the crisis, began to integrate these models into their risk assessment protocols. By simulating a wide range of market scenarios, including those characterized by extreme volatility, firms could better gauge potential exposures and tail risks in their portfolios. This shift marked a move towards more stress-tolerant and robust risk management strategies, acknowledging the unpredictable nature of markets.

An essential aspect of employing stochastic models effectively lies in their calibration to real market data. Post-2008, the emphasis on accurate model calibration intensified, with financial modelers leveraging advanced computational techniques and optimization algorithms. Calibration processes involve adjusting model parameters to align with market prices of derivatives, thus ensuring the models' outputs are as realistic as possible. Techniques such as the Kalman Filter and Bayesian inference have been pivotal in refining the calibration process, thereby enhancing the predictive power and reliability of stochastic models.

The insights gleaned from stochastic volatility models have also profoundly impacted trading strategies. Traders, equipped with models that offer a deeper understanding of volatility's erratic nature, have been able to develop more sophisticated strategies that can adapt to and capitalize on market inefficiencies. Moreover, the ability of these models to forecast extreme market movements has enabled the crafting of hedging strategies that provide better protection against unforeseen market downturns.

As we venture further into the 21st century, the quest for more refined stochastic volatility models continues. The integration of machine learning techniques with traditional stochastic modeling approaches offers promising avenues for capturing the multifaceted nature of market volatility. Researchers and practitioners are exploring the use of artificial neural networks, for instance, to predict volatility patterns based on a broader spectrum of market indicators and sentiment analysis.

The analysis of volatility patterns through the lens of stochastic models represents a critical area of focus in the post-2008 financial landscape. These models have not only enriched our understanding of market dynamics but also revolutionized risk management and trading strategies. As financial markets continue to evolve, so too will the models we rely on to navigate their complexities. The journey of refining and applying stochastic volatility models is ongoing, mirroring the perpetual movement and unpredictability of the markets they seek to decode.

Lessons Learned and the Role of Quantitative Modeling Post-Crisis

One of the most salient lessons to emerge from the crisis was the inherent danger in over-relying on quantitative models without accounting for their limitations and potential blind spots. Pre-crisis, the pervasive confidence in models like the Black-Scholes, which assumed constant volatility and market efficiency, led to underestimation of systemic risks. The post-crisis era, therefore, marked a paradigm shift towards acknowledging the models' assumptions and stress-testing these assumptions against extreme market scenarios.

The aftermath of the crisis catalyzed significant

advancements in quantitative modeling, with a concerted effort to bridge the gap between theoretical elegance and practical applicability. Stochastic volatility models, recognizing the dynamic nature of volatility, became central to this new era of model development. The introduction of models capable of capturing the leptokurtic nature of market returns—exhibiting fat tails and a peaked center—allowed for a more accurate representation of market risk.

A key lesson from the crisis was the critical importance of tail risk—the risk of extreme market movements that lie outside the normal distribution curve. Financial institutions now integrate tail risk considerations into their strategic decision-making processes, employing quantitative models that explicitly account for such extremes. This has led to the development of more resilient financial products and investment strategies that can withstand market shocks.

The financial crisis also prompted a global overhaul of financial regulations, with initiatives like the Dodd-Frank Act in the United States and the Basel III framework internationally. In this new regulatory environment, quantitative modeling has assumed a pivotal role in ensuring compliance, particularly in stress testing and risk management processes. Models now need to satisfy regulatory requirements for transparency, robustness, and the ability to simulate adverse market conditions, thereby fostering a safer financial system.

The limitations exposed by the crisis have opened the door to interdisciplinary approaches that incorporate insights from behavioral finance into quantitative models. Recognizing that market movements are not always rational but are influenced by human behavior, models now increasingly account for psychological factors. Furthermore, the integration of machine learning and artificial intelligence offers the potential to analyze vast datasets, identifying patterns and correlations beyond human cognitive capabilities, thus enhancing the sophistication of quantitative models.

The lessons learned from the 2008 financial crisis have profoundly reshaped the role of quantitative modeling in finance. The crisis served as a stark reminder of the complexities and unpredictabilities inherent in financial markets, driving innovation and adaptation in quantitative modeling. Today, these models are more robust, more nuanced, and better equipped to navigate the financial landscape. The evolution of quantitative modeling post-crisis reflects a maturation of the field, embracing both the power and the limits of mathematical and statistical approaches in understanding financial markets. As we move forward, the continual refinement and adaptation of these models will remain essential in the quest to balance risk and reward in an ever-changing financial world.

7 The Flash Crash and Other Market Anomalies

The fabric of financial markets is occasionally torn by sudden, inexplicable events that defy the expectations set by traditional models. These phenomena, known as market anomalies, pose significant challenges to the foundational assumptions of financial theory. Among these, the Flash Crash of May 6, 2010, stands as a watershed moment, a stark illustration of the market's vulnerability to complex, high-frequency trading algorithms.

On that unforgettable day, the Dow Jones Industrial Average plunged nearly 1,000 points in mere minutes, erasing almost

$1 trillion in market value before a bafflingly rapid recovery. This event spotlighted the fragility of financial markets in the digital age, where high-frequency trading (HFT) algorithms can amplify market movements through rapid, voluminous transactions.

Investigations into the Flash Crash uncovered a confluence of factors, with a significant emphasis on the role of HFT and the interconnectedness of modern trading platforms. An initial sell-off in E-Mini S&P 500 index futures triggered a cascade of automated trading activities, which, in a tightly coupled market ecosystem, led to a liquidity vacuum and exacerbated the crash.

The Flash Crash served as a critical lesson on the potential perils of algorithmic trading when not adequately checked by risk management practices. It underscored the need for more robust market safeguards, including circuit breakers and liquidity requirements, to prevent future occurrences. Moreover, it called into question the reliability of quantitative models that failed to anticipate such extreme events, highlighting the importance of incorporating systemic risk and feedback loops into financial modeling.

In the aftermath of the Flash Crash, stochastic volatility models have been revised to better capture the dynamics of market anomalies. These models now often include parameters that account for sudden shifts in market liquidity and investor sentiment, aiming to provide a more comprehensive framework for understanding and predicting market behavior.

Furthermore, the event has spurred interest in developing models that can simulate the impact of algorithmic trading on market stability. By incorporating the strategies and behaviors of HFT algorithms, these models strive to predict and mitigate the potential triggers of future market anomalies.

While the Flash Crash is emblematic, it is but one instance in a series of market anomalies that challenge traditional financial models. Other events, such as the sudden spike in Swiss Franc exchange rates in 2015 and periodic liquidity crises in bond markets, emphasize the need for a broader understanding of market behavior. These events illustrate the market's susceptibility to geopolitical events, policy changes, and the evolving landscape of financial technology.

Detailed Case Study of the 2010 Flash Crash

the Flash Crash was a large sell order on the E-Mini S&P 500 futures contracts, executed via an automated algorithmic trading strategy. This strategy, designed to minimize market impact, instead served as the catalyst for an unprecedented sell-off. The algorithm's decision to unload a significant volume of contracts in a short time, without regard to price or time, triggered a domino effect.

HFT algorithms, programmed to detect and exploit patterns in market orders, began to aggressively sell in anticipation of further declines, exacerbating the downward spiral. This rapid selling pressure created a feedback loop, where price declines triggered more selling, leading to what is known as a liquidity vacuum. As liquidity evaporated, the market's ability to absorb the shock was compromised, leading to a freefall in prices.

In the aftermath, a joint report by the Securities and Exchange Commission (SEC) and the Commodity Futures Trading

Commission (CFTC) pinpointed the lack of synchronized trading pauses across markets as a critical vulnerability. The disparate rules and triggers for halting trading allowed the volatility to cascade through markets unchecked.

In response, regulatory bodies implemented a series of reforms aimed at enhancing market stability. These included the introduction of cross-market circuit breakers designed to halt trading temporarily in the event of extreme price movements, giving traders time to reassess their positions and reducing the likelihood of panic-induced selling.

The Flash Crash also prompted a reevaluation of stochastic volatility models. Traditional models, which often assume market efficiency and rationality, were ill-equipped to account for the behavioral anomalies and feedback loops exposed by the crash. This has led to the development of more sophisticated models that incorporate variables for market sentiment, liquidity conditions, and the potential impact of algorithmic trading strategies.

These enhanced models seek to capture the non-linear dynamics of markets under stress, offering a more nuanced understanding of risk and the potential for extreme events. They represent an evolving toolkit for traders, risk managers, and regulators alike, in their quest to navigate and safeguard against the inherent unpredictabilities of financial markets.

The 2010 Flash Crash stands as a stark reminder of the fragility of financial markets in the face of technology-driven trading. It highlights the need for continuous vigilance, adaptability in regulatory frameworks, and advancements in quantitative modeling to understand and mitigate systemic risks.

As markets evolve, so too does the sophistication of the technologies and strategies deployed within them. The ongoing challenge for the financial community is to ensure that innovation in market practices is matched by equally innovative approaches to risk management and regulation. The Flash Crash is not merely a lesson from the past; it is a cautionary tale for the future, emphasizing the importance of preparedness for the unforeseeable dynamics of global financial markets.

Using Stochastic Volatility Models to Understand and Simulate Market Anomalies

Market anomalies represent instances where financial markets deviate from expected norms, often marked by extreme volatility and unpredictable behavior. Traditional models, based on the assumption of constant volatility, fall short in capturing the essence of these events. Stochastic volatility models, by contrast, incorporate time-varying volatility and the potential for sudden shifts in market sentiment, making them particularly adept at simulating these anomalies.

One of the seminal models in this domain, the Heston model, introduces stochastic variance with mean reversion, capturing the tendency of volatility to fluctuate around a long-term average. This characteristic is crucial in modeling market anomalies, where volatility can spike dramatically but eventually returns to a baseline level.

The simulation of market anomalies using stochastic volatility models involves numerical methods that can handle the complexity of these models. Monte Carlo simulation, for instance, is widely used for its flexibility in modeling diverse scenarios. By generating a multitude of potential future market paths, it allows for the exploration of the outer bounds of market behavior, including extreme events like market crashes.

For example, to simulate an event akin to the Flash Crash, one could adjust the parameters of the Heston model to reflect higher volatility and faster mean reversion, representative of the rapid price movements and subsequent recovery observed during the crash. Through simulation, one can observe not just the price dynamics but also the potential triggers and market conditions that could lead to such anomalies.

Applying stochastic volatility models to the Flash Crash, researchers can dissect the event beyond the surface level of large sell orders and algorithmic trading feedback loops. By simulating the market conditions leading up to May 6, 2010, including the build-up of positions by high-frequency trading algorithms and the subsequent liquidity crisis, stochastic models offer insights into the confluence of factors that precipitated the crash.

These simulations can also test the effectiveness of regulatory measures implemented post-crash, such as cross-market circuit breakers. By modeling scenarios with and without these safeguards, stochastic volatility models help in assessing their potential to mitigate the impact of similar future anomalies.

The integration of machine learning with stochastic volatility models represents the cutting edge in simulating and understanding market anomalies. Machine learning algorithms can analyze vast datasets to identify patterns and correlations that precede market anomalies, enhancing the predictive power of stochastic models.

For instance, a machine learning model could analyze historical market data to identify precursors to liquidity crises. These insights could then inform the parameters of a stochastic volatility model, refining its ability to simulate scenarios that lead to market anomalies.

Stochastic volatility models, bolstered by numerical simulation and machine learning, offer a powerful toolset for understanding the multifaceted nature of market anomalies. While no model can predict every anomaly with certainty, the continued refinement of these models moves us closer to a future where financial markets are not only better understood but also more resilient in the face of the unpredictable.

By simulating the conditions that lead to market anomalies, we gain not only insights into past events but also the foresight to navigate the complexities of future market dynamics. In this endeavor, stochastic volatility models remain an indispensable asset, evolving in step with the markets they seek to decode.

Discussion on the Resilience of Financial Markets and Algorithmic Trading

Market resilience refers to the ability of financial systems to continue to operate effectively even when faced with significant stressors, such as market anomalies or economic downturns. In this context, algorithmic trading emerges as both a boon and a bane. On one hand, algorithms can enhance market liquidity and efficiency, executing trades at speeds and volumes unattainable by human traders. On the other, they can exacerbate market volatility, as seen in events like the Flash Crash, where rapid sell-offs by algorithms led to a temporary but dramatic market plunge.

The dual nature of algorithmic trading necessitates a nuanced understanding of its impact on market resilience. Stochastic volatility models, with their capacity to simulate complex market behaviors under varying conditions, serve as invaluable tools in this endeavor. By adjusting model parameters to reflect different levels of algorithmic trading activity, researchers can assess how changes in trading patterns might affect market stability.

To dissect the relationship between algorithmic trading and market resilience, it's essential to consider the mechanisms through which algorithms operate. High-frequency trading (HFT) algorithms, for instance, can provide liquidity by continuously placing buy and sell orders. In stable market conditions, this can lead to tighter spreads and more efficient price discovery. However, during times of stress, these algorithms may quickly withdraw, draining liquidity and amplifying price movements.

Stochastic volatility models can simulate these scenarios, providing insights into the conditions under which algorithmic trading enhances or erodes market resilience. For example, by incorporating variables that mimic the withdrawal of HFT liquidity in response to certain triggers, models can forecast potential impacts on market stability.

Regulatory bodies worldwide recognize the double-edged sword of algorithmic trading and have taken steps to mitigate its risks without stifling its benefits. Measures such as circuit breakers, which temporarily halt trading when prices move too quickly, aim to prevent the kind of rapid spirals seen in past market anomalies. Stochastic volatility models play a role here as well, offering a sandbox for testing the effectiveness of different regulatory strategies in maintaining market resilience.

Moreover, these models can help regulators and market participants understand the conditions under which algorithmic trading contributes positively to market dynamics. By identifying such conditions, it's possible to design trading rules and algorithms that bolster, rather than weaken, market resilience.

As financial markets continue to evolve, so too must the models we use to understand them. The integration of machine learning with stochastic volatility models offers a pathway to more accurately predict and manage the impact of algorithmic trading on market resilience. Machine learning can uncover subtle patterns and relationships in market data that traditional models might miss, facilitating the development of more robust trading algorithms.

Furthermore, fostering a culture of innovation and collaboration among traders, regulators, and academics is crucial for enhancing market resilience. By sharing insights and exploring new modeling techniques, stakeholders can collectively work toward a financial ecosystem that is not only efficient and dynamic but also capable of withstanding the shocks and stresses of an unpredictable world.

the discussion on the resilience of financial markets and the role of algorithmic trading highlights the complex, intertwined nature of modern financial ecosystems. Stochastic volatility models, enriched with cutting-edge computational techniques, offer a powerful lens through which to examine and enhance this resilience. As we look to the future, the continuous refinement of these models, along with thoughtful regulatory and technological innovation, will be key to navigating the complexities and uncertainties of global financial markets.

COVID-19 and Market Volatility

The onset of the COVID-19 pandemic in early 2020 led to a seismic shift in global financial markets. As countries around the world grappled with the health crisis, markets plunged into turmoil, with stock indices experiencing their fastest falls in history. This period of intense volatility was not only a reflection of the immediate economic uncertainty but also a test of market structures and mechanisms in the face of a global shock.

Stochastic volatility models, enhanced with pandemic-specific variables, have been pivotal in analyzing these market dynamics. By incorporating factors such as infection rates, lockdown measures, and fiscal stimulus announcements, these models offer insights into the direct and indirect effects of the pandemic on financial markets. The ability to simulate various scenarios has helped in understanding the sensitivity of markets to different pandemic-related developments.

A significant aspect of the COVID-19 market saga was the swift and substantial response from governments and central banks worldwide. From interest rate cuts and quantitative easing to unprecedented fiscal stimulus packages, these actions aimed to stabilize financial markets and cushion the economic fallout. Stochastic volatility models provide a framework for assessing the effectiveness of these interventions, illustrating how they influenced market sentiment and volatility patterns.

By adjusting model inputs to reflect specific policy measures, one can evaluate their impact on reducing volatility and restoring investor confidence. This analysis highlights the critical role of timely and targeted government action in mitigating market disruptions during a crisis.

The pandemic also brought about significant changes in investor behavior, marked by a shift towards digital trading platforms and a rise in retail investor participation. These behavioral changes have implications for market volatility and liquidity, as demonstrated by the increased trading volumes and the rapid price movements of certain stocks favored by retail investors.

Stochastic volatility models that account for changes in trading behavior and investor sentiment can shed light on these phenomena. By modeling the increased influence of retail investors and the proliferation of digital trading, one can explore their contributions to market volatility during the pandemic.

The COVID-19 pandemic has underscored the importance of adaptability and resilience in financial markets. Stochastic volatility models, with their ability to simulate a wide range of scenarios, emerge as essential tools for preparing for future shocks. These models can help market participants and regulators identify vulnerabilities and develop strategies to enhance market stability.

Furthermore, the pandemic experience highlights the need for continuous innovation in modeling techniques. Integrating machine learning and big data analytics with traditional stochastic volatility models can improve the accuracy of volatility forecasts and the understanding of complex market dynamics in crisis situations.

In reflecting on the COVID-19 pandemic and its impact on market volatility, it becomes apparent that sophisticated modeling approaches are crucial for navigating such unprecedented events. Stochastic volatility models, enriched with contemporary data and advanced analytics, offer a pathway to understanding and managing the complexities of pandemic-induced market shocks. As we move forward, the lessons learned from this crisis will be invaluable in strengthening the resilience of financial markets against future global challenges, ensuring they are better equipped to withstand and recover from extreme volatility.

Impact of the COVID-19 Pandemic on Global Financial Markets

The initial outbreak of COVID-19 triggered a domino effect across global financial markets. Equity markets plummeted, erasing trillions of dollars in value within weeks, as investors scrambled to assess the potential economic fallout. This period witnessed extreme spikes in market volatility, far surpassing the levels observed during the 2008 financial crisis. Stochastic volatility models, calibrated to capture the rapid escalation in uncertainty, have been instrumental in dissecting these initial reactions, revealing how the interplay between fear and uncertainty fueled the market downturn.

As the pandemic unfolded, it precipitated a reevaluation of traditional investment strategies. Investors, faced with a landscape of negative interest rates and uncertain returns, began to diversify their portfolios beyond conventional asset classes. Cryptocurrencies and tech stocks, for instance, saw remarkable surges in value, reflecting a shift towards assets perceived as hedges against inflation and economic instability.

Stochastic volatility models, adapted to account for these shifts, illustrate the changing risk profiles and the increased importance of dynamic asset allocation. These models have proven crucial in navigating the investment landscape during the pandemic, enabling investors to recalibrate their strategies in response to evolving market conditions.

The COVID-19 pandemic has also accelerated changes in market infrastructure and trading behaviors. The surge in online trading platforms and algorithmic trading has been notable, as lockdown measures and social distancing norms pushed more investors towards digital finance solutions. This shift has implications for market liquidity and volatility, with stochastic volatility models highlighting the increased frequency and magnitude of price swings associated with algorithm-driven trades.

Furthermore, the pandemic has underscored the critical role of robust market infrastructure in maintaining trading continuity and integrity. Upgrades to electronic trading systems, enhancements in clearing and settlement processes, and the adoption of cloud-based solutions have emerged as key priorities, ensuring that markets can operate efficiently even in the face of significant disruptions.

Looking beyond the immediate crisis, the COVID-19 pandemic is likely to leave a lasting imprint on global financial markets. The acceleration of digital transformation, the reevaluation of risk management frameworks, and the potential for regulatory reforms are among the long-term outcomes that stakeholders must navigate.

Stochastic volatility models, evolving with these shifts, offer a valuable tool for forecasting future market dynamics and for stress-testing portfolios against a range of scenarios. By incorporating insights from the pandemic, these models can help investors, regulators, and policymakers prepare for a new era in financial markets, characterized by greater digital integration, heightened volatility, and an expanded toolkit for managing financial risks.

The COVID-19 pandemic has catalyzed profound changes in global financial markets, from immediate market reactions to long-term strategic shifts. Stochastic volatility models, by capturing the essence of these changes, provide a framework for understanding and adapting to the new market paradigm. As the world gradually emerges from the shadow of the pandemic, these insights will be instrumental in navigating the complexities of an ever-evolving financial landscape, ensuring that stakeholders are better equipped to face future challenges with resilience and foresight.

Modeling Pandemic-Induced Volatility Shocks

The volatility induced by the COVID-19 pandemic is distinguished by its sudden onset, global reach, and the simultaneous impact on multiple asset classes. Traditional models, which often presuppose a degree of market efficiency and rationality, found themselves ill-equipped to handle the erratic movements triggered by the pandemic. The challenge, therefore, lies in developing stochastic volatility models that can accommodate the non-linear dynamics and fat-tailed distributions characteristic of such black swan events.

The adaptation of stochastic volatility models to better handle pandemic-induced shocks has involved several key innovations. One approach has been to integrate jump-diffusion processes, which allow for sudden, significant changes in asset prices, thereby capturing the sharp market downturns and recoveries observed during the pandemic. Models such as the Heston model have been extended to include jump components, enhancing their ability to simulate the erratic market behavior seen in early 2020.

Another significant development has been the incorporation of macroeconomic indicators into stochastic models. By linking volatility to real-world events such as lockdowns, stimulus announcements, and infection rates, these enhanced models offer a more nuanced understanding of the drivers behind market movements. This approach facilitates the creation of more accurate risk assessments and stress testing scenarios, enabling investors and policymakers to make informed decisions in the face of uncertainty.

The modeling of pandemic-induced volatility has also benefited from advanced quantitative techniques, including machine learning and Bayesian inference. Machine learning algorithms, with their ability to process vast datasets and identify complex patterns, have been instrumental in predicting volatility spikes and their subsequent impacts on asset prices. Bayesian methods, on the other hand, offer a probabilistic framework for updating model parameters in real-time, as new information about the pandemic and its economic effects becomes available.

One notable application of these techniques is in the calibration of stochastic volatility models to market data. The calibration process, crucial for ensuring the models' accuracy and predictive power, has been challenged by the pandemic's unpredictable nature. Machine learning and Bayesian inference have provided the tools necessary to dynamically adjust model parameters, thereby maintaining their relevance in rapidly changing market conditions.

Despite the advancements in modeling pandemic-induced volatility, several challenges remain. The primary issue is the scarcity of historical data on similar events, which complicates the model calibration and validation processes. Additionally, the global interconnectedness of modern financial markets means that regional events can have far-reaching effects, adding another layer of complexity to volatility modeling.

Looking ahead, the focus will be on developing more robust and adaptive stochastic volatility models that can withstand the test of extreme market conditions. This will involve not only the refinement of existing models and techniques but also the exploration of new paradigms in financial mathematics and computational finance. The lessons learned from modeling the COVID-19 pandemic will undoubtedly play a critical role in shaping the future of volatility modeling, ensuring that the financial world is better prepared for the next black swan event.

This detailed examination of pandemic-induced volatility modeling underscores the importance of innovation, adaptability, and interdisciplinary approaches in navigating the challenges posed by extreme market conditions. As we continue to refine these models, the goal remains clear: to enhance our understanding of financial market dynamics and improve our readiness for future uncertainties.

Adapting Trading Strategies to "Black Swan" Events

The first and foremost adaptation involves embracing strategic flexibility. Traders have learned the hard way that rigid trading strategies, which perform well under normal market conditions, can lead to significant losses during Black Swan events. The pandemic has highlighted the necessity for strategies that are not only robust but also adaptable, capable of quickly responding to sudden market changes.

One approach to achieving this flexibility is through the incorporation of real-time data analytics into trading decisions. By leveraging state-of-the-art technology and machine learning algorithms, traders can now analyze market data as it unfolds, identifying emerging trends and adjusting their positions accordingly. This real-time responsiveness is crucial for navigating the volatility characteristic of Black Swan events.

Another key adaptation has been the broadening of diversification strategies to include non-traditional asset classes. The pandemic has demonstrated that correlations between asset classes can shift dramatically in times of crisis, undermining the protective power of traditional diversification. In response, savvy traders are exploring assets previously considered peripheral, such as cryptocurrencies, commodities, and even non-fungible tokens (NFTs), to construct portfolios that are more resilient to the shocks of Black Swan events.

The strategic use of options has also gained prominence as a method for managing the risks associated with extreme market volatility. Options provide a way to hedge against unfavorable price movements while allowing traders to benefit from market upswings. During the COVID-19 pandemic, the intelligent use of options strategies, such as protective puts and covered calls, has enabled traders to navigate market turbulence more effectively, protecting their portfolios from severe downturns.

A renewed emphasis on liquidity and capital preservation has become a cornerstone of trading strategies adapted for Black Swan events. The rapid market declines seen during the pandemic have underscored the importance of maintaining sufficient liquidity to cover margin calls and avoid forced liquidation. Traders have become more circumspect about leverage, prioritizing the preservation of capital over the pursuit of high returns. This conservative approach ensures that traders can withstand prolonged periods of market instability and capitalize on recovery opportunities when they arise.

Lastly, adapting to Black Swan events requires a commitment to continuous learning and scenario planning. The unprecedented nature of the COVID-19 pandemic has revealed gaps in the collective knowledge of financial markets and their behavior under extreme stress. Forward-thinking traders are investing in education and technology that enable them to simulate various market scenarios, including worst-case scenarios, to better prepare for future uncertainties.

The adoption of these adaptive strategies represents a paradigm shift in the approach to trading in the face of Black Swan events. By prioritizing flexibility, diversification, risk management, liquidity, and continuous learning, traders can not only safeguard their investments but also identify and leverage the unique opportunities such events invariably present. As the financial landscape continues to evolve, the lessons learned from the COVID-19 pandemic will undoubtedly shape trading strategies for years to come, making the markets more resilient and traders more adept at navigating the unknown.

CHAPTER 8: IMPLEMENTING PYTHON SOLUTIONS FOR REAL-WORLD FINANCE

An Automated Trading System is a computer program that creates orders and automatically submits them to a market center or exchange. The system operates on predefined algorithms and trading strategies without the need for manual intervention. The algorithms are based on a myriad of inputs including, but not limited to, market prices, technical indicators, and economic statistics.

The architecture of an ATS is built on a foundation of rigorous data analysis and backtesting. The initial step involves formulating a trading hypothesis based on historical market data. Python, with its rich ecosystem of libraries such as pandas for data manipulation, NumPy for numerical computations, and Matplotlib for visualization, is an ideal programming language for this task.

Following hypothesis formulation, the strategy undergoes

backtesting — a process where the strategy is applied to historical data to ascertain its viability. This phase is critical, as it allows the developer to refine the strategy by tweaking parameters and eliminating biases, thereby enhancing its robustness.

Once a strategy has been backtested and validated, it transitions into the implementation phase. Here, the algorithm is coded into a functional trading system. This process requires a seamless integration of the trading logic with a brokerage's execution API to facilitate real-time trading. Python's requests library or specialized brokerage libraries, such as IBPy for Interactive Brokers, are instrumental in accomplishing this task.

The operational mechanics of an ATS are governed by its trading algorithms, which can range from simple moving average crossovers to complex machine learning models that predict market movements. The choice of algorithm significantly influences the system's performance and is largely contingent on the trader's risk appetite and trading style.

An integral component of an ATS is risk management. This involves setting predefined criteria for trade entries and exits, position sizing, and stop-loss orders to mitigate losses. Python's capabilities for mathematical computation enable the development of sophisticated risk management algorithms that can dynamically adjust to market conditions.

Automated Trading Systems have transformed the landscape of financial markets in several ways. By executing trades at high speeds, they enhance market liquidity and efficiency. Moreover, they have democratized the trading arena, enabling retail investors to employ strategies that were once the preserve of institutional traders.

However, the proliferation of ATS has not been without its challenges. Issues such as market flash crashes, attributed to high-frequency trading algorithms, have sparked debates on the need for regulatory oversight.

The future of Automated Trading Systems is inextricably linked to advancements in technology and finance. Emerging trends include the integration of machine learning and artificial intelligence to develop self-learning trading algorithms that adapt to changing market conditions. Furthermore, the advent of blockchain technology and decentralized finance (DeFi) presents new avenues for ATS, potentially redefining trading strategies in the years to come.

Automated Trading Systems represent a pivotal innovation in financial trading, harnessing the power of technology to execute complex strategies with precision and efficiency. As the field continues to evolve, the convergence of finance, technology, and regulation will shape the future trajectory of automated trading, promising to unlock new potentials and challenges alike.

Design and Implementation of an Automated Trading System Using Python

The journey of creating an ATS begins with a conceptual framework that outlines the trading strategy's core premise. It involves identifying the market inefficiencies or patterns the system aims to exploit. This phase is critical as it sets the direction for the subsequent technical development and dictates the data requirements for backtesting the strategy.

Python shines in data acquisition and preprocessing with libraries such as pandas and NumPy facilitating efficient data manipulation. For an ATS, historical market data forms the backbone of strategy development. This data can be sourced from various APIs like Alpha Vantage, Quandl, or directly from exchanges, depending on the granularity required. Preprocessing involves cleaning the data, handling missing values, and formatting the data into a structure suitable for analysis and backtesting.

With clean data at hand, the next step involves translating the conceptual framework into a quantifiable strategy. This is where Python's versatility is invaluable. Libraries such as pandas for data manipulation and TA-Lib for technical indicators allow for the exploration of different strategy hypotheses.

Backtesting is a pivotal phase in the ATS development process. It involves simulating the strategy on historical data to evaluate its performance. Python's backtrader library offers a powerful yet flexible framework for backtesting, providing insights into the strategy's profitability, risk metrics, and potential for overfitting.

Translating a backtested strategy into a live ATS requires careful attention to detail. The implementation phase covers the coding of the strategy into a script that can interact with the market in real-time. This involves integrating the script with a brokerage's API for order execution. The python-requests library or specific brokerage SDKs facilitate this connectivity, allowing the ATS to place trades based on real-time data.

Risk management is coded into this phase, ensuring the ATS adheres to predefined risk parameters. This includes setting stop-loss levels, position sizing, and diversification rules to mitigate losses and protect the trading capital.

Deploying an ATS in a live market environment is the culmination of the design and implementation process. However, deployment is not the end. Continuous monitoring is essential to ensure the system operates as intended, to adjust parameters as market conditions change, and to identify any anomalies in trading behavior.

Deployment can benefit from cloud computing services like AWS or Google Cloud to ensure the system runs with high uptime and low latency, critical for strategies sensitive to execution speed.

While building an ATS, ethical considerations and regulatory compliance must be at the forefront. This includes ensuring the system does not engage in market manipulation practices and adheres to the trading rules of the platforms and jurisdictions it operates within.

Designing and implementing an Automated Trading System using Python is a complex but rewarding endeavor that combines the fields of finance, programming, and data science. Through careful planning, rigorous backtesting, and continuous monitoring, it is possible to develop an ATS that not only automates trading but does so with a strategic edge in the market. As the landscape of financial technology evolves, so too will the methodologies and capabilities of automated trading systems, offering ever-greater opportunities and challenges for developers and traders alike.

Integrating Stochastic Volatility Models for Signal Generation

Stochastic volatility models lies the recognition that market volatility is not constant but varies over time in a random, yet somewhat predictable manner. Models such as Heston and SABR have become cornerstones in understanding and quantifying this dynamism, offering a mathematical framework that captures the essence of market volatility movements. By integrating these models into the signal generation process, traders can gain a more nuanced understanding of market conditions, enhancing the predictive power of their trading strategies.

Stochastic volatility models thrive on quality data. In the context of an ATS, both historical and real-time market data streams are vital. Historical data allows for the calibration of the model, tuning it to capture the idiosyncrasies of specific financial instruments or markets. Real-time data, on the other hand, feeds into the model during live trading operations, enabling the ATS to adapt its strategies based on current market conditions.

Python, with libraries like pandas and NumPy, excels in handling these data requirements, allowing for efficient storage, manipulation, and analysis. Preliminary analysis often involves statistical exploration of historical data to understand volatility patterns, an essential step before model integration.

Calibration is a critical step in preparing stochastic volatility models for signal generation. It involves adjusting model parameters so that the model's output aligns with observed market prices and volatility patterns. Python's optimization libraries, such as SciPy, play a pivotal role in this process, offering various algorithms to minimize the difference between model predictions and actual market observations.

Once calibrated, the integration of the stochastic volatility model into the ATS encompasses embedding the model within the trading logic. This integration enables the ATS to utilize volatility forecasts as part of its decision-making framework. For instance, a model predicting an increase in volatility might trigger strategies designed to profit from higher market movements, adjusting positions accordingly.

The signal generation process, enriched by stochastic volatility models, becomes a sophisticated ensemble of market analysis and prediction. Signals can be generated based on thresholds defined within the model's output, such as volatility levels expected to precede market rallies or downturns. Python's ability to process complex calculations in real-time allows these models to operate within the high-speed environment of an ATS, ensuring signals are timely and actionable.

Incorporating machine learning techniques, such as reinforcement learning, can further refine the signal generation process. By learning from past performance, the ATS can adjust its strategies based on the success rate of signals generated with the integration of stochastic volatility models, fostering a continuously evolving trading system.

Backtesting remains an indispensable phase, evaluating the effectiveness of integrating stochastic volatility models into signal generation. Python's backtrader library offers a comprehensive environment for simulating trading strategies against historical data, allowing for the assessment of performance metrics and risk factors. Optimization at this stage focuses on fine-tuning model parameters and trading thresholds to maximize profitability while managing risk.

The integration of stochastic volatility models into the signal generation of Automated Trading Systems represents a frontier in algorithmic trading, offering enhanced foresight and adaptability in navigating financial markets. Python, with its rich ecosystem of libraries and frameworks, stands as an ideal platform for implementing these complex models, providing traders with cutting-edge tools to refine their strategies. As financial markets continue to evolve, the synergy between stochastic volatility models and automated trading systems will undoubtedly deepen, heralding new paradigms in algorithmic trading.

Performance Evaluation and Risk Management

The evaluation of an ATS's performance, particularly one that integrates sophisticated stochastic volatility models, begins with the establishment of clear, quantifiable metrics. These metrics often include total return, Sharpe ratio, Sortino ratio, and drawdown characteristics. Each metric offers insights into different facets of the system's profitability and risk-adjusted performance.

- Total Return measures the system's profitability over a specified period, offering a straightforward assessment of its effectiveness in capital appreciation.

- Sharpe Ratio evaluates the excess return per unit of risk, providing a lens through which the risk-adjusted return can be gauged. A higher Sharpe ratio indicates a more desirable outcome, where returns are achieved with less risk.

- Sortino Ratio, similar to the Sharpe ratio but focusing solely on downside risk, offers a refined view of the risk-adjusted return, especially relevant in strategies sensitive to downward market movements.

- Drawdown Characteristics examine the magnitude and duration of peak-to-trough declines during a specific period. This metric is crucial in understanding the potential for losses and the system's ability to recover from downturns.

Python, with its vast array of libraries such as pandas for data manipulation and matplotlib for visualization, provides an ideal environment for calculating these metrics. Through concise scripts, traders can automate the performance evaluation process, gaining rapid insights into their systems' efficacy.

Risk management, in its essence, is the practice of identifying, assessing, and prioritizing risks followed by the coordinated application of resources to minimize or control the probability and/or impact of unfortunate events. Within the context of an ATS that leverages stochastic volatility models, risk management transcends traditional boundaries, incorporating sophisticated methodologies to preempt and mitigate financial risk.

- Value at Risk (VaR) and Conditional Value at Risk (CVaR) stand as the cornerstones of modern risk management strategies. VaR estimates the maximum loss over a target horizon at a specific confidence level, while CVaR provides the expected loss exceeding the VaR threshold.

- Stress Testing involves simulating the ATS under extreme market conditions, often historical or hypothetical scenarios, to assess its resilience against market shocks.

- Sensitivity Analysis delves into how changes in market conditions affect the performance of the trading system, providing insights into potential vulnerabilities.

Python's scipy and numpy libraries are instrumental in implementing these risk management techniques, allowing for complex simulations and analyses that are pivotal in crafting robust financial safeguards.

The interplay between performance evaluation and risk management is pivotal in the domain of quantitative trading. It's not merely about maximizing returns but doing so within a framework that judiciously manages risk. By integrating stochastic volatility models, traders can endow their ATS with a nuanced understanding of market dynamics, enabling more informed trading decisions. However, the robustness of these systems is contingent upon rigorous performance evaluation and a comprehensive risk management framework.

Using Python for both performance evaluation and risk management imbues the trading system with a level of dynamism and adaptability essential for navigating the complex waters of financial markets. It allows for real-time adjustments based on performance metrics and risk assessments, ensuring that the system remains aligned with its objectives while safeguarding against market volatilities.

Performance evaluation and risk management are inseparable companions in the journey of algorithmic trading. They provide the metrics for success and the mechanisms for protection, guiding the ATS towards its goal of profitability. In the context of stochastic volatility models, these practices gain even greater prominence, acting as the linchpins that secure the model's potential within a framework of calculated risk and measured success. Through the adept use of Python, traders can navigate these practices with precision, ensuring that their trading strategies are both potent and protected in the face of market uncertainties.

Portfolio Optimization and Management

Portfolio optimization is a systematic approach aimed at selecting the best assortment of assets, in terms of expected return and risk, to achieve a desired investment objective. it seeks to maximize returns for a given level of risk or, conversely, to minimize risk for a given level of expected return. This optimization process is underpinned by the efficient frontier concept, which defines the set of optimal portfolios offering the highest expected return for a defined level of risk or the lowest risk for a given level of expected return.

- Modern Portfolio Theory (MPT) lays the foundation for portfolio optimization, emphasizing diversification to reduce risk. MPT posits that an investor can construct a portfolio of multiple assets that will yield higher returns than individual assets for a given level of risk through diversification.

- Stochastic Volatility Models enhance MPT by providing a more nuanced understanding of the risk associated with each asset in the portfolio. By modeling the unpredictable nature of volatility, these models enable investors to make more informed decisions regarding asset selection and allocation.

Python, with its rich ecosystem of libraries such as NumPy for numerical computations and SciPy for optimization algorithms, serves as an invaluable tool for implementing portfolio optimization strategies. Pandas library is particularly useful for handling financial data, allowing for efficient manipulation and analysis critical in the optimization process.

Portfolio management involves the ongoing process of constructing and adjusting a portfolio to meet specific investment goals, taking into consideration factors such as risk tolerance, investment horizon, and market conditions. Effective portfolio management strategies include:

- Asset Allocation: Determining the optimal distribution of assets based on the investor's risk tolerance and investment objectives. This strategy balances the portfolio across different asset classes (e.g., stocks, bonds, real estate) to mitigate risk.

- Rebalancing: Periodically adjusting the portfolio to maintain the desired level of asset allocation. Market movements can shift the initial allocation, necessitating rebalancing to realign the portfolio with the investor's objectives.

- Use of Derivatives: Incorporating financial instruments such as options and futures to hedge against market volatility and protect the portfolio from downside risks.

Python's flexibility and computational power enable the

implementation of complex portfolio management strategies. For instance, the use of Monte Carlo simulations, facilitated by Python's libraries, allows for the modeling of various market scenarios to test portfolio resilience and inform rebalancing decisions.

The incorporation of stochastic volatility models into portfolio optimization and management represents a significant advancement in handling financial data's inherent uncertainty. These models provide a more realistic representation of market conditions, enabling more accurate predictions of asset price movements and correlations.

- Calibration to Market Data: Python's optimization libraries can be employed to calibrate stochastic volatility models to historical market data, ensuring that the models accurately reflect current market dynamics.

- Risk Assessment: By simulating thousands of possible future market conditions, stochastic volatility models offer comprehensive risk assessments, enabling investors to identify and mitigate potential portfolio risks.

Portfolio optimization and management are pivotal in navigating the complexities of the financial markets, aiming at maximizing returns while controlling for risk. The integration of stochastic volatility models, powered by Python's computational capabilities, offers a sophisticated approach to understanding and managing the unpredictable nature of financial markets. Through strategic asset allocation, regular rebalancing, and the prudent use of derivatives, investors can achieve a well-optimized and managed portfolio that aligns with their investment goals, all while leveraging the cutting-edge advancements in quantitative finance methodologies.

Using Python for Dynamic Portfolio Optimization

Unlike static portfolio optimization that takes a snapshot approach to asset allocation, dynamic portfolio optimization is akin to navigating a rapidly flowing river, requiring constant adjustments and recalibrations to maintain the desired investment course. It involves:

- Continuous Monitoring: Keeping a vigilant eye on market changes and portfolio performance to identify when adjustments are needed.

- Adaptive Strategies: Implementing strategies that can quickly respond to market volatility, economic shifts, and changes in the investor's financial goals or risk tolerance.

Python's role in this dynamic environment is crucial. Its extensive libraries and frameworks enable the rapid processing of vast datasets and the execution of complex algorithms essential for real-time decision-making.

Real-time market data analysis is the cornerstone of dynamic portfolio optimization. Python, through libraries such as pandas for data manipulation and matplotlib for data visualization, offers a robust platform for:

- Data Ingestion: Automating the process of fetching real-time financial data from various sources.

- Data Processing: Cleaning, transforming, and analyzing the data to extract actionable insights.

- Visualization: Creating interactive charts and graphs to visualize trends and patterns that inform decision-making.

Stochastic volatility models account for the random nature of markets and the uncertainty inherent in financial data. Python's NumPy and SciPy libraries are invaluable for implementing these models, allowing for the simulation of asset price movements under different market scenarios. Key aspects include:

- Model Calibration: Utilizing Python's optimization functions to fit the models to current market data, ensuring predictions are grounded in the latest market dynamics.

- Risk Management: Applying Monte Carlo simulations to assess the risk associated with various portfolio configurations under stochastic market conditions.

Dynamic portfolio optimization requires sophisticated algorithms that can find the optimal asset allocation efficiently. Python's SciPy library offers a range of optimization algorithms, including:

- Constrained Optimization: Ensuring that portfolio adjustments meet specific constraints, such as minimum risk or target return.

- Genetic Algorithms: Exploring a variety of portfolio configurations to identify the optimal allocation through a process that mimics natural selection.

These algorithms are pivotal in navigating the complex landscape of dynamic portfolio optimization, enabling the development of strategies that can adapt to market changes swiftly and efficiently.

The ultimate goal of using Python for dynamic portfolio optimization is to facilitate real-time decision-making. This involves:

- Automated Trading: Developing Python scripts that can execute trades automatically based on predefined criteria, ensuring the portfolio remains optimized without constant manual intervention.

- Alert Systems: Implementing alert mechanisms that notify investors of significant market events or when portfolio adjustments are advisable.

Dynamic portfolio optimization represents a sophisticated approach to investment management, demanding a high level of adaptability and responsiveness to market changes. Python, with its powerful computational capabilities and extensive ecosystem of libraries, stands as an indispensable tool for investors seeking to implement dynamic portfolio optimization strategies. Through real-time data analysis, stochastic model implementation, and the use of advanced optimization algorithms, Python enables the construction of adaptive, resilient portfolios poised to capitalize on opportunities and mitigate risks in the ever-evolving financial markets.

Stochastic Models for Assessing Portfolio Risk and Return

In the domain of quantitative finance, the assessment of portfolio risk and return through stochastic models is a nuanced endeavor that intertwines probability theory with financial instruments. This detailed exploration delves into the crux of using stochastic models to gauge the performance and potential pitfalls inherent in diversified portfolios.

- Geometric Brownian Motion (GBM): The GBM model represents a pillar in financial modeling, assuming lognormal price movements over time. It forms the basis of the Black-Scholes model for option pricing, extending its application to portfolio risk management by evaluating possible future values of assets under varying market conditions.

- Mean-Reverting Models: Contrasting the GBM, mean-reverting models such as the Ornstein-Uhlenbeck process assume that asset prices tend to revert to a long-term mean. This property is particularly pertinent in strategies involving fixed-income securities and commodities, where price levels may oscillate around equilibrium values.

- Jump-Diffusion Models: Incorporating sudden, significant changes in asset prices, jump-diffusion models add a layer of realism by accounting for market shocks or events leading to abrupt price adjustments. These models are crucial for stress-testing portfolios against extreme market movements.

The quintessence of risk management lies in understanding and preparing for variability in portfolio returns. Stochastic models enable the quantification of this variability through metrics such as Value at Risk (VaR) and Conditional Value at Risk (CVaR), providing insights into potential losses under adverse market conditions.

- Value at Risk (VaR): Utilizing the Monte Carlo simulation, a stochastic model-driven approach, VaR estimates the maximum potential loss of a portfolio over a specified timeframe with a given confidence interval. This metric offers a clear, probabilistic assessment of risk, aiding in the strategic allocation of assets to minimize potential downturns.

- Conditional Value at Risk (CVaR): Going beyond VaR, CVaR delves into the tail risks, calculating the expected losses in the worst-case scenarios beyond the VaR threshold. It offers a more comprehensive view of extreme risk, guiding more resilient portfolio construction.

Beyond risk assessment, stochastic models are instrumental in optimizing portfolios for enhanced returns. Through the stochastic optimization process, investors can identify the asset allocation that maximizes expected returns for a given level of risk, incorporating the random nature of future asset performances.

- Efficient Frontier and Stochastic Optimization: The stochastic models contribute to plotting an efficient frontier that delineates the optimal trade-off between risk and return. By simulating numerous possible future states of the world, stochastic optimization techniques identify the portfolio compositions lying on this frontier, enabling investors to make informed decisions aligned with their risk tolerance and return expectations.

While the theoretical underpinnings are robust, the practical application of stochastic models in portfolio management confronts several challenges. The accuracy of these models depends significantly on the assumptions made regarding market dynamics and asset behavior. Moreover, the calibration of model parameters to historical data, while necessary, may not always capture future market conditions accurately. Investors and portfolio managers must remain cognizant of these limitations, adopting a judicious approach to model selection and parameterization.

Stochastic models for assessing portfolio risk and return represent a critical tool in the arsenal of quantitative finance. By encapsulating the complex, probabilistic nature of financial markets, these models offer a structured approach to navigating the uncertainties of investment. Through careful application and ongoing refinement, stochastic modeling facilitates informed decision-making, enabling the construction of portfolios that adeptly balance risk and return in alignment with investor objectives.

Techniques for Diversification and Efficient Frontier Analysis

Diversification stands as a cornerstone principle in risk management and portfolio optimization. At its essence, diversification involves spreading investments across various assets or asset classes to reduce exposure to the risk inherent in any single investment. The goal is to construct a portfolio that yields the highest possible return for a given level of risk, or conversely, the lowest risk for a given level of return.

- Asset Allocation: The first step in diversification is determining the optimal asset allocation, which involves selecting a mix of asset classes (e.g., stocks, bonds, real estate) in proportions that align with the investor's risk appetite and return objectives. Strategic asset allocation leverages historical performance data and future expectations to balance the portfolio across these classes.

- Sector and Geographic Diversification: Beyond asset classes, diversification extends to investing across different sectors (technology, healthcare, finances) and geographies (domestic, emerging markets). This approach mitigates sector-specific and region-specific risks, capitalizing on growth opportunities in varied economic environments.

Efficient frontier analysis, rooted in Modern Portfolio Theory (MPT), provides a powerful quantitative framework for realizing diversification's full potential. It involves plotting a set of optimal portfolios that offer the highest expected return for a given level of risk or the lowest risk for a given level of return.

- Construction of the Efficient Frontier: Utilizing historical returns, volatilities, and correlations among the assets, one can compute the expected return and variance for a plethora of portfolio compositions. The efficient frontier is the graphical representation of these portfolios, forming a curve on a risk-return plot where no portfolio can offer higher returns without increased risk.

- Optimization Algorithms: The advent of computational finance has facilitated the use of sophisticated optimization algorithms to calculate the efficient frontier. Techniques such as quadratic programming and Monte Carlo simulations enable investors to sift through the vast array of possible portfolios to identify those lying on the efficient frontier.

- Selection of Optimal Portfolio: With the efficient frontier established, investors can pinpoint the optimal portfolio that aligns with their specific risk-return profile. This might involve selecting a portfolio with the maximum Sharpe ratio, which signifies the highest return per unit of risk.

- Dynamic Rebalancing: Market conditions and asset correlations evolve, causing the efficient frontier to shift. Regular portfolio rebalancing, guided by efficient frontier analysis, ensures that the portfolio remains optimized in alignment with the investor's objectives and market realities.

While diversification and efficient frontier analysis are theoretically sound, their practical application requires careful consideration. Market anomalies, changes in asset correlations during market stress, and transaction costs can all impact the effectiveness of these strategies. Moreover, the reliance on historical data to project future returns and risks is a significant limitation, as past performance is not always indicative of future results.

Employing techniques for diversification and efficient frontier analysis equips investors with a robust framework for constructing portfolios that adeptly balance the trade-off between risk and return. By integrating these strategies within their investment process, investors can navigate the complexities of the financial markets with increased confidence and clarity. However, the dynamic nature of markets necessitates continuous learning, adaptation, and a pragmatic approach to model assumptions and data analysis. Through such diligence, the pursuit of investment excellence becomes a structured, yet flexible journey towards financial optimization.

Regulatory Compliance and Risk Reporting

Regulatory compliance encompasses adherence to laws, regulations, guidelines, and specifications relevant to financial operations. These regulatory frameworks are designed to protect investors, ensure market fairness, and mitigate systemic risk. They vary significantly across jurisdictions, reflecting differences in market structures, investor profiles, and historical financial crises experiences.

- Global and Local Regulations: Key regulatory bodies such as the U.S. Securities and Exchange Commission (SEC), the Financial Conduct Authority (FCA) in the UK, and the European Securities and Markets Authority (ESMA) set the stage for a global regulatory landscape. Financial institutions must also navigate local regulations, demanding a nuanced understanding of compliance requirements across operational geographies.

- Regulatory Acts and Directives: Prominent regulatory frameworks include the Dodd-Frank Act in the United States, MiFID II in Europe, and Basel III international banking regulations. These regulations encompass a wide range of financial activities, from trading practices to capital requirements and corporate governance.

Risk reporting is an integral component of an institution's risk management framework, providing insights into various risk exposures and the effectiveness of risk mitigation strategies. Effective risk reporting enables timely decision-making and is crucial for regulatory compliance.

- Quantitative and Qualitative Reporting: Risk reports typically include both quantitative metrics, such as Value at Risk (VaR), and qualitative assessments of risk factors. These reports must strike a balance between comprehensiveness and clarity, ensuring that key risk insights are accessible to stakeholders.

- Regular and Ad-hoc Reporting: Institutions engage in regular reporting cycles, often dictated by regulatory requirements, as well as ad-hoc reporting in response to significant risk events or market changes. The agility in reporting mechanisms is vital for adapting to emerging risks.

The implementation of regulatory compliance and risk reporting strategies involves a multifaceted approach, combining technology, data analytics, and organizational culture.

- Technology and Data Infrastructure: Advanced data management and analytics platforms are essential for handling the volume and complexity of regulatory and risk reporting requirements. These systems must ensure data accuracy, integrity, and timeliness.

- Organizational Culture: Cultivating a culture of compliance and risk awareness across all levels of the organization is fundamental. This involves training, clear communication of risk management policies, and embedding risk considerations into strategic decision-making processes.

- Continuous Adaptation: Regulatory landscapes and risk profiles are dynamic. Institutions must remain vigilant, continuously updating their compliance and reporting frameworks to reflect new regulations, market developments, and emerging risks.

Navigating regulatory compliance and risk reporting is fraught with challenges, including the pace of regulatory change, technological advancements, and the evolving nature of financial risks. Future directions may involve increased reliance on artificial intelligence and machine learning for predictive risk analytics, blockchain for transparent and secure reporting, and collaborative efforts among regulators and industry participants to harmonize regulatory standards.

The Importance of Regulatory Compliance in Finance

Regulatory compliance in finance is not just about adhering to a set of rules; it's about upholding the principles that ensure markets function efficiently, transparently, and fairly. Compliance frameworks are designed to prevent fraud, market manipulation, and unethical behavior that could erode investor confidence and disrupt market equilibrium.

- Investor Protection: regulatory compliance serves to protect investors from misleading practices and financial harm. This protection is crucial for maintaining investor trust, which is the lifeblood of financial markets. By ensuring that financial institutions operate transparently and in the best interest of their clients, regulatory compliance safeguards the interests of both individual and institutional investors.

- Preventing Systemic Risk: The financial crisis of 2008 underscored the domino effect that the failure of a single entity can have on the global financial system. Compliance with regulatory standards on capital adequacy, liquidity, and risk management is essential for mitigating systemic risk. These standards ensure that financial institutions can withstand financial shocks and contribute to the overall stability of the financial system.

Regulatory compliance plays a pivotal role in fostering an environment conducive to sustainable economic growth. By setting the ground rules for fair competition and financial innovation, regulatory frameworks help stimulate economic development while managing potential risks.

- Fair Competition: Regulatory compliance ensures that all market participants operate on a level playing field, preventing monopolistic practices and fostering healthy competition. This competitive landscape encourages innovation, efficiency, and diversity in financial services, contributing to economic dynamism and resilience.

- Encouraging Financial Innovation: While regulations set boundaries for financial activities, they also provide a structured environment in which innovation can thrive. Compliance with regulatory standards encourages institutions to innovate within these frameworks, leading to the development of new financial products, services, and technologies that can drive economic growth.

The landscape of financial regulations is constantly evolving, reflecting changes in market dynamics, technological advancements, and lessons learned from financial crises. Financial institutions must remain agile, adapting their compliance strategies to meet both current and future regulatory requirements.

- Global Coordination: In an increasingly interconnected world, financial markets transcend national borders, necessitating coordinated regulatory efforts across jurisdictions. International regulatory bodies and agreements play a crucial role in harmonizing standards, reducing the potential for regulatory arbitrage, and fostering global financial stability.

- Leveraging Technology for Compliance: Technological advancements, including regulatory technology (RegTech), offer powerful tools for enhancing compliance efficiency and effectiveness. By leveraging big data analytics, artificial intelligence, and blockchain, financial institutions can streamline compliance processes, improve risk management, and stay ahead of regulatory changes.

Using Python to Automate Risk Reporting and Compliance Processes

The shift towards automation in risk reporting and compliance is driven by the need for real-time analysis, precision in risk assessment, and adherence to an ever-growing body of regulatory requirements. Python, with its extensive libraries and user-friendly syntax, emerges as a frontrunner in facilitating this transition.

- Streamlining Data Collection: effective risk reporting lies the aggregation and analysis of vast datasets. Python's libraries, such as Pandas and NumPy, simplify data collection, manipulation, and cleansing, enabling compliance officers to consolidate information from disparate sources with ease.

- Enhancing Analytical Capabilities: Python's powerful analytical libraries, including SciPy and StatsModels, allow for sophisticated risk modeling and simulations. These capabilities enable institutions to identify potential risks and vulnerabilities with greater accuracy, informing more strategic decision-making processes.

- Automating Reporting Functions: The generation of compliance and risk reports is a recurring task that demands precision and consistency. Python scripts can automate the creation of these reports, ensuring that they are generated accurately and efficiently. Libraries like Matplotlib and Seaborn facilitate the inclusion of visual analytics in reports, enhancing their comprehensibility and impact.

To illustrate the practical application of Python in automating risk reporting and compliance processes, consider the example of automating the generation of a risk exposure report.

1. Data Aggregation: Utilize Python's Pandas library to import and consolidate data from various sources, such as internal databases and market data feeds. This step involves cleaning the data to rectify any inconsistencies or missing values.

```python

import pandas as pd

# Load data from multiple sources

market_data = pd.read_csv('market_data.csv')

internal_positions = pd.read_excel('internal_positions.xlsx')

# Merge datasets
```

```
consolidated_data          =          pd.merge(market_data,
internal_positions, on='asset_id')
```

` ` `

2. Risk Analysis: Apply statistical models to assess the portfolio's exposure to various risk factors. This can involve calculating Value-at-Risk (VaR), stress testing, or scenario analysis. Python's SciPy library offers functions for statistical analysis and modeling.

` ` `python

```
from scipy.stats import norm

# Assuming a simplified VaR calculation for demonstration

portfolio_mean = consolidated_data['position_value'].mean()

portfolio_std = consolidated_data['position_value'].std()

VaR_95 = norm.ppf(0.05, portfolio_mean, portfolio_std)

print(f"Value-at-Risk (95% confidence): {VaR_95}")
```

` ` `

3. Report Generation: Automate the reporting process using Python to create structured reports. This includes textual

summaries, tables, and graphical representations of risk exposures.

```python
import matplotlib.pyplot as plt

# Plotting portfolio risk exposure

consolidated_data['position_value'].plot.hist(bins=20, alpha=)

plt.title('Portfolio Risk Exposure')

plt.xlabel('Position Value')

plt.ylabel('Frequency')

plt.savefig('portfolio_risk_exposure.png')

```

4. Compliance Verification: Ensure that the portfolio's risk exposure complies with regulatory limits and internal risk guidelines. Python can be used to automate checks against these criteria, flagging any deviations for further review.

```python
regulatory_limit = 100000
```

```
if VaR_95 > regulatory_limit:
```

```
print("Risk exposure exceeds regulatory limit. Further review required.")
```

```
else:
```

```
print("Risk exposure within acceptable limits.")
```

```
` ` `
```

Stochastic Models in Stress Testing and Scenario Analysis

Stress testing and scenario analysis are analytical methods used by financial institutions to assess how certain stress conditions or hypothetical scenarios could impact their operations, assets, or investments. While stress testing focuses on understanding the impact of extreme market events, scenario analysis explores a wider range of possible future events, including changes in market conditions, sudden economic downturns, or geopolitical crises.

- Stress Testing: Typically involves modeling extreme but plausible adverse conditions to assess the financial institution's vulnerability. The aim is to ensure that the institution has adequate capital and strategies in place to withstand shocks.

- Scenario Analysis: Provides a more comprehensive approach, examining the impact of various hypothetical scenarios on an institution's financial position. This includes both adverse and positive developments, allowing for a more rounded view of potential risks and opportunities.

Stochastic models are integral to both stress testing and scenario analysis, providing the mathematical framework necessary to simulate the wide array of possible future states of the market or economic conditions. These models take into account the randomness and volatility inherent in financial markets, allowing for a more nuanced understanding of risk.

1. Modeling Market Dynamics: At the core of stochastic models is the simulation of market variables such as interest rates, stock prices, and foreign exchange rates. By applying stochastic differential equations, these models can generate realistic market behavior under various conditions.

```python
import numpy as np

# Simulating a Geometric Brownian Motion (GBM) for stock prices

def simulate_gbm(S0, mu, sigma, T, steps):

dt = T/steps

t = np.linspace(0, T, steps)

W = np.random.standard_normal(size=steps)
```

W = np.cumsum(W)*np.sqrt(dt) # the Wiener process

X = (mu-*sigma2)*t + sigma*W

S = S0*np.exp(X) # GBM formula

return t, S

```
```

2. Conducting Stress Tests: Stochastic models enable the simulation of extreme but plausible market conditions to assess the impact on a portfolio's value. This involves altering model inputs to reflect adverse conditions and observing the outcomes.

```python

T = 1  # Time in years

S0 = 100  # Initial stock price

mu = 0.05  # Expected return

sigma =  # Volatility

steps = 250  # Number of steps

# Simulating adverse market conditions with increased
```

volatility

t, stressed_prices = simulate_gbm(S0, mu, sigma*1.5, T, steps)

```
```

3. Scenario Analysis: By varying the parameters within stochastic models, analysts can explore a wide range of scenarios, from mild to severe, and gauge the potential impacts on financial health and regulatory compliance.

```python

# Exploring a scenario with a significant drop in expected returns

t, scenario_prices = simulate_gbm(S0, mu*, sigma, T, steps)

```
```

The insights gleaned from applying stochastic models in stress testing and scenario analysis are invaluable for strategic planning and risk management. They guide financial institutions in capital allocation, risk mitigation strategies, and in formulating responses to potential market disruptions. Moreover, these models assist in demonstrating compliance with regulatory requirements, showcasing an institution's preparedness for adverse financial conditions.

Stochastic models are indispensable tools in the arsenal of financial risk management, offering the sophistication and
```

flexibility necessary to navigate the uncertainties of the financial landscape. Through stress testing and scenario analysis, these models illuminate the path forward, enabling institutions to brace for storms on the horizon and seize opportunities in volatility. As we venture further into the realms of quantitative finance, the exploration and enhancement of stochastic modeling techniques will continue to be paramount in mastering the art of risk management.

CHAPTER 9: BEYOND TRADITIONAL MARKETS: CRYPTOCURRENCIES AND DERIVATIVES

Cryptocurrency markets are renowned for their extreme fluctuations. This volatility is not merely a function of market sentiment but is deeply ingrained in the very fabric of the cryptocurrency ecosystem. Several factors contribute to this phenomenon, including limited liquidity, the nascent stage of the market's development, and the often speculative nature of investments. Furthermore, news and social media play a disproportionate role in shaping investor sentiment, leading to rapid price movements.

To understand this volatility, one must appreciate the underlying technology—blockchain—and the process of price discovery in markets that operate 24/7 across diverse regulatory landscapes. Unlike traditional markets with set trading hours, cryptocurrencies are traded around the clock, exposing them to continuous news cycles and event-driven spikes in volatility.

Quantitative models for analyzing volatility in cryptocurrency markets often adapt techniques from traditional financial markets but must account for the unique characteristics of digital assets. Stochastic volatility models, while widely used in equities and commodities markets, require modification to capture the leptokurtic (heavy-tailed) distribution of cryptocurrency returns.

One approach is to utilize a variant of the Heston model, modified for the high kurtosis and skewness observed in cryptocurrency returns. This involves calibrating the model to reflect the rapid adjustments in variance, capturing the swift shifts in market sentiment typical of cryptocurrencies.

For traders and investors, understanding and navigating volatility in cryptocurrency markets is crucial. The use of stochastic volatility models enables the construction of strategies that can adapt to the market's dynamic environment. For instance, option pricing models tailored to cryptocurrencies allow for more accurate hedging strategies, helping to manage risk in highly volatile portfolios.

Moreover, algorithmic trading strategies can be designed to exploit volatility patterns. By simulating various scenarios using stochastic models, traders can identify optimal entry and exit points, maximizing returns while mitigating undue risk. These strategies often incorporate machine learning algorithms to refine predictions and adjustments based on real-time market data.

While stochastic volatility models offer powerful tools for understanding cryptocurrency markets, several challenges remain. Model calibration is particularly complex, given the lack of historical data compared to more established markets. Additionally, the rapid pace of innovation in blockchain technology and regulatory changes can swiftly alter market dynamics, requiring constant model adjustments.

Furthermore, the decentralized nature of many cryptocurrency exchanges introduces additional layers of risk, including security concerns and the potential for market manipulation. These factors must be meticulously considered when developing trading strategies based around volatility modeling.

The volatility of cryptocurrency markets, while daunting, presents a fertile ground for the application of advanced stochastic volatility models. By carefully adapting models from traditional finance and integrating machine learning algorithms, traders can navigate the complexities of these digital marketplaces. The key lies in a nuanced understanding of the market's drivers, continuous model refinement, and a proactive approach to risk management. As the cryptocurrency market matures, so too will the sophistication of the strategies designed to harness its volatility, opening new frontiers in financial modeling and trading strategy development.

Characteristics of Cryptocurrency Markets and Volatility

cryptocurrency markets is the principle of decentralization. Unlike traditional financial markets governed by central authorities, cryptocurrencies operate on decentralized networks, primarily blockchain technology. This foundational characteristic introduces a level of market fragmentation unseen in conventional markets. With hundreds of exchanges operating globally without a centralized pricing mechanism, disparities in liquidity and price across platforms contribute significantly to overall market volatility.

Liquidity, or the lack thereof, plays a critical role in the volatility of cryptocurrency markets. Many digital assets are traded on exchanges with varying degrees of liquidity, meaning that significant transactions can lead to substantial price swings. This situation is exacerbated in the case of altcoins (alternative cryptocurrencies to Bitcoin), where lower trading volumes can lead to even more pronounced volatility. The relationship between liquidity and volatility is cyclical, with the former directly impacting the price stability of digital assets.

Cryptocurrency markets are heavily influenced by speculative trading, with investors often driven by short-term gains rather than the underlying value of the assets. This speculative nature contributes to rapid price movements, as traders react swiftly to news, rumors, and social media trends. The speculative bubble phenomenon, clearly observed in the dramatic rise and fall of prices, underscores the market's sensitivity to speculative trading activities.

The regulatory landscape for cryptocurrencies remains undefined in many jurisdictions, contributing to market instability. Regulatory announcements can lead to abrupt market reactions, as traders and investors adjust their strategies based on perceived risks and opportunities. This uncertainty is a key driver of volatility, with the potential for significant regulatory changes to either stabilize or destabilize the market depending on their nature and scope.

The relentless pace of technological advancements in the cryptocurrency space introduces both opportunities and challenges. Innovations such as new consensus mechanisms, scaling solutions, and decentralized finance (DeFi) applications can rapidly shift market dynamics, influencing volatility. While these developments hold the promise of enhancing efficiency and broadening the utility of cryptocurrencies, they also introduce new variables into the market, impacting price and volatility.

The decentralized and digital nature of cryptocurrencies means that information flows rapidly and can be disseminated widely through social media and news outlets. This immediacy of information contributes to the market's reactive nature, with prices often moving swiftly in response to news, whether substantiated or not. The phenomenon of 'FOMO' (fear of missing out) further amplifies volatility, as traders rush to buy or sell based on the latest trends and news stories.

Understanding the characteristics of cryptocurrency markets and the drivers of their volatility is essential for both participants and observers. The interplay of decentralization, liquidity, speculative trading, regulatory uncertainty, technological advancements, and information flow creates a market environment that is inherently volatile. This volatility presents both risks and opportunities, requiring a nuanced approach to navigate successfully. As the market continues to mature, it will be fascinating to observe how these dynamics evolve and what new characteristics will emerge in the ever-changing landscape of cryptocurrency markets.

Stochastic Volatility Models Tailored to Cryptocurrencies

The unpredictable and often extreme fluctuations in cryptocurrency prices demand models capable of capturing rapid shifts in volatility. Traditional models, while foundational, require modifications to address the idiosyncrasies of the crypto markets. One adaptation involves the incorporation of heavy-tailed distributions and jump-diffusion processes into the models. Cryptocurrencies frequently experience sudden, significant price movements (jumps) that traditional Gaussian-based models may inadequately capture. Integrating jump components allows for a more accurate representation of these abrupt changes in price.

Cryptocurrency markets are markedly influenced by investor sentiment, news, and social media trends. Stochastic volatility models tailored to cryptocurrencies often integrate sentiment analysis to gauge the market's emotional temperature. By analyzing data from news articles, social media posts, and search trends, these models can incorporate the impact of investor sentiment on volatility. This integration helps in predicting volatility spikes triggered by events or news, providing a more nuanced understanding of market dynamics.

The leverage effect, a phenomenon where price drops lead to increased volatility, is pronounced in cryptocurrency markets. Models tailored for cryptocurrencies often incorporate asymmetric volatility features, where the model's parameters adjust differently to price rises and falls. This asymmetry captures the observed behavior in crypto markets, where negative news or events tend to have a more significant impact on volatility compared to positive developments.

Cryptocurrency markets operate round-the-clock, generating vast amounts of high-frequency data. This continuous trading produces microstructure noise, complicating the extraction of meaningful volatility signals. Tailored stochastic volatility models address this by applying filtering techniques or adopting models specifically designed for high-frequency data. These models strive to isolate genuine market signals from noise, enhancing the accuracy of volatility estimates.

Calibrating stochastic volatility models to cryptocurrency markets poses significant challenges due to the markets' inefficiencies, liquidity variations, and regulatory uncertainties. Advanced calibration techniques, including Bayesian inference and machine learning algorithms, are employed to tackle these challenges. These methods can handle the complex, nonlinear relationships inherent in crypto markets, adjusting model parameters dynamically as new data becomes available.

The practical application of tailored stochastic volatility models in cryptocurrency markets spans risk management, derivative pricing, and strategic trading decisions. These models enable traders and investors to assess the risk of their positions more accurately, price options and futures, and devise hedging strategies to mitigate unexpected losses. However, it's crucial to acknowledge the limitations of these models, including their dependency on historical data, which may not always predict future volatility patterns accurately, especially in a market as young and rapidly evolving as the cryptocurrency sector.

The tailoring of stochastic volatility models to cryptocurrency markets represents a dynamic and field of quantitative finance. By addressing the unique challenges of these digital assets, the adapted models offer valuable tools for understanding and navigating the complexities of cryptocurrency volatility. As the market matures and more data becomes available, these models will continue to evolve, enhancing their predictive power and applicability to the burgeoning world of cryptocurrencies.

Trading and Risk Management Strategies for Cryptocurrencies

Cryptocurrency trading strategies often start with a fundamental analysis of market conditions, including the broader economic indicators, sentiment analysis, and the technological underpinnings of the assets themselves. However, given the significant impact of market sentiment and news on cryptocurrency prices, traders increasingly leverage technical analysis and algorithmic trading techniques. These methods include trend following, mean reversion strategies, and arbitrage opportunities, exploiting the inefficiencies inherent in the fragmented cryptocurrency markets.

Algorithmic trading, using computer algorithms to execute trades at speeds and volumes that are impossible for humans, plays a pivotal role in cryptocurrency trading. These algorithms can process market data, execute trades based on predefined criteria, and adjust strategies in real-time. High-frequency trading (HFT) algorithms, for example, capitalize on minute price discrepancies across exchanges. Meanwhile, machine learning models predict price movements by analyzing vast datasets, including market trends, transaction volumes, and social media sentiment.

The cornerstone of successful cryptocurrency trading lies in effective risk management. Given the asset's volatility, traders employ various techniques to protect their investments. Stop-loss orders, a fundamental risk management tool, limit potential losses by automatically selling assets when prices fall below a predetermined level. Position sizing strategies ensure that no single trade can significantly impact the overall portfolio, while diversification across different cryptocurrencies and asset classes spreads risk.

Hedging, a strategy designed to reduce risk by taking offsetting positions, is crucial in the cryptocurrency context. Options and futures contracts on cryptocurrencies allow traders to hedge against adverse price movements effectively. For instance, buying put options on Bitcoin provides the right to sell at a predetermined price, offering protection against price drops. Similarly, futures contracts enable traders to lock in prices for future transactions, mitigating the risk of price volatility.

Derivatives, including options and futures, are integral to managing the risks associated with cryptocurrency investments. These financial instruments enable traders to speculate on price movements without holding the underlying asset, offering opportunities for leverage and hedging. The use of derivatives must be approached with caution, as the leverage they provide can amplify losses just as it can magnify gains.

Liquidity, or the ease with which an asset can be bought or sold in the market without affecting its price, is a critical factor in cryptocurrency trading. High liquidity facilitates smoother trades and less slippage, reducing the cost of entering and exiting positions. Traders manage liquidity risk by choosing highly liquid markets for larger trades and employing algorithms that can detect and exploit liquidity in fragmented markets.

Effective trading is not just about algorithms and strategies; it's also about managing one's emotions and psychological responses to market movements. The fear of missing out (FOMO) can drive irrational trading decisions, as can panic selling during market downturns. Successful traders maintain discipline, adhering to their strategies and risk management principles even in the face of volatility.

Trading and managing risk in the cryptocurrency markets require a sophisticated blend of quantitative analysis, technological tools, and psychological discipline. By employing a comprehensive suite of strategies—ranging from algorithmic trading and hedging to rigorous risk management techniques—traders can navigate the volatile cryptocurrency markets with greater confidence and effectiveness. As the market continues to evolve, so too will the strategies, requiring constant learning and adaptation to stay ahead.

Derivatives and Structured Products

Derivatives are financial contracts whose value is derived from the performance of an underlying asset, index, or rate. These instruments, including futures, options, and swaps, serve crucial functions in global markets for hedging risks, speculating on price movements, and arbitraging price discrepancies between markets. they offer market participants the leverage to amplify their exposure to market movements without the need to directly hold the underlying asset.

Structured products, a nuanced class of financial instruments, are engineered to cater to specific investor needs that cannot be met with standard derivatives. These products are synthesized from a combination of derivatives and other assets to provide tailored risk-return profiles. Often, structured products are crafted to offer capital protection, enhanced returns, or access to otherwise inaccessible markets or assets. The allure of structured products lies in their flexibility and the bespoke investment solutions they offer, albeit at the cost of increased complexity and reduced liquidity.

The nascent yet rapidly evolving cryptocurrency markets present fertile ground for the application of derivatives and structured products. Given the inherent volatility and speculative nature of cryptocurrencies, derivatives like futures and options have become indispensable tools for traders and investors. These instruments enable market participants to hedge against adverse price swings in their cryptocurrency holdings and to speculate on future movements with a defined risk profile.

Futures contracts on Bitcoin and other leading cryptocurrencies, traded on platforms such as the Chicago Mercantile Exchange (CME), have seen growing adoption. Similarly, options on cryptocurrencies are offering traders the flexibility to implement sophisticated strategies that were once reserved for traditional financial markets.

Structured products come into play in offering retail and institutional investors exposure to cryptocurrency performance without the direct risks of holding the assets. These products can include principal-protected notes with exposure to a basket of cryptocurrencies or yield enhancement products that offer higher returns in exchange for taking on certain market risks.

Successful navigation of the derivatives and structured

products landscape requires a deep understanding of both the instruments and the underlying market dynamics. Traders and investors must adeptly manage the leverage and risk these instruments entail, ensuring strategies are aligned with their investment objectives and risk tolerance.

For instance, using options to create straddles or strangles allows traders to profit from significant moves in cryptocurrency prices, regardless of the direction. Meanwhile, structured products can be designed to provide downside protection while still participating in upside potential, appealing to investors with a more cautious outlook.

The regulatory environment surrounding derivatives and structured products, especially in the cryptocurrency space, is under continuous development. Participants must stay abreast of legal and regulatory changes that could impact the pricing, availability, and attractiveness of these instruments.

Moreover, as technology advances and the cryptocurrency market matures, new derivatives and structured products are likely to emerge. These innovations will further expand the toolbox available to traders and investors, enabling more nuanced and sophisticated strategies.

Derivatives and structured products represent a critical dimension of financial markets, offering mechanisms for risk management, speculation, and investment diversification. In the volatile and burgeoning field of cryptocurrency trading, these instruments are indispensable. Mastery over derivatives and structured products empowers market participants to navigate the complexities of the financial landscape with precision, leveraging their potential for strategic advantage while mitigating inherent risks. As the markets for these instruments evolve, staying informed and adaptable will be paramount for sustained success.

Overview of Derivatives and Their Role in Modern Finance

In the web of modern finance, derivatives stand as pivotal instruments, facilitating a myriad of strategic operations ranging from risk management to speculative ventures. This segment aims to dissect the essence of derivatives, offering a panoramic view of their functions, the mechanics behind their operation, and their indispensable role within the financial ecosystem.

a derivative is a financial contract, the value of which is pegged to an underlying asset or set of assets. These underlying assets can be diverse, including stocks, bonds, commodities, currencies, interest rates, or market indexes. The most common forms of derivatives are futures, options, forwards, and swaps, each with distinct characteristics and applications.

Futures and Forwards: These contracts obligate the buyer to purchase, and the seller to sell, an asset at a predetermined future date and price. While futures are standardized and traded on exchanges, forwards are customized agreements traded over-the-counter (OTC).

Options: Options provide the holder the right, but not the obligation, to buy (call options) or sell (put options) the underlying asset at a specified price before or at the contract's expiration. They offer asymmetrical payoffs, allowing for strategies that can profit from both market ups and downs.

Swaps: Swaps are agreements between two parties to exchange

cash flows or other financial instruments over a specified time. The most common types are interest rate swaps and currency swaps, crucial for managing fluctuations in interest rates and exchange rates, respectively.

One of the paramount roles of derivatives lies in their capacity for risk management or hedging. Financial markets are fraught with uncertainties, and derivatives offer a mechanism to lock in prices, effectively insulating market participants from adverse price movements in the underlying assets. For instance, an airline company might use fuel futures to hedge against the risk of rising jet fuel prices, ensuring budget predictability.

Beyond hedging, derivatives are potent tools for speculation. Speculators utilize derivatives to bet on the future direction of market prices with the objective of profiting from price movements. The leverage inherent in derivatives means that significant returns can be achieved from relatively small initial investments. However, this comes with commensurately high risk, as losses can also be magnified.

Derivatives enable arbitrageurs to profit from price discrepancies in different markets or forms. By simultaneously buying and selling equivalent assets in different markets, arbitrageurs can exploit these discrepancies for risk-free profit, contributing to market efficiency by ensuring prices do not deviate significantly from their fair value.

Derivatives have a profound influence on the liquidity and efficiency of financial markets. They add depth to the markets by providing more trading opportunities and vehicles for risk sharing, which, in turn, enhances market liquidity.

Furthermore, the pricing of derivatives involves sophisticated models and analyses, contributing to more accurate pricing of risk and underlying assets in the broader market.

While derivatives are invaluable tools in finance, their complexity and leverage also make them sources of systemic risk, as evidenced by historical financial crises. The opacity of OTC derivatives markets and the interconnectedness they foster among financial institutions have prompted regulatory bodies worldwide to implement more stringent regulations to mitigate these risks.

Derivatives are integral to the modern financial landscape, offering flexibility, efficiency, and opportunities for market participants across the spectrum. Their ability to facilitate risk management, provide leverage for speculation, and create arbitrage opportunities underscores their pivotal role. However, navigating the derivatives market demands a sophisticated understanding of both financial instruments and market forces, highlighting the need for prudent management and regulatory oversight to harness their benefits while mitigating inherent risks.

Applying Stochastic Volatility Models to Price Complex Derivatives

Stochastic volatility models are predicated on the notion that market volatility is not constant but varies in a random fashion over time. Unlike the classical Black-Scholes model, which assumes a fixed volatility, stochastic volatility models introduce a second stochastic process to model volatility itself. This additional layer of complexity allows for a more accurate representation of market dynamics, encompassing the leptokurtic nature of asset returns and the volatility smile

—a pattern observed in the implied volatilities of options across different strikes.

The Heston model is a seminal example in this category, characterized by its tractability and the relative ease with which it can be calibrated to market data. It models the asset price and its variance as two correlated stochastic processes, thereby capturing the essential features of financial markets more effectively than its constant-volatility counterparts.

Complex derivatives, such as exotic options, barrier options, and options with path-dependent features, require sophisticated pricing models that can accommodate their unique characteristics. The Heston model, with its stochastic volatility framework, is particularly adept at this task.

Consider the pricing of a European call option under the Heston framework. The model allows for the explicit calculation of the option's price by integrating the probability density functions of the asset's price and volatility over time. This integration is performed using numerical methods such as the Fast Fourier Transform (FFT), which significantly accelerates the computation.

Moreover, the correlation parameter between the asset's price and its volatility in the Heston model introduces the leverage effect—an empirical observation where asset returns are negatively correlated with changes in volatility. This feature is crucial for accurately pricing derivatives that are sensitive to the skewness and kurtosis of return distributions.

The application of stochastic volatility models like the Heston model in pricing complex derivatives offers several advantages:

- Enhanced Accuracy: By accounting for the dynamic nature of volatility, these models yield prices that are more aligned with observed market values, particularly for long-dated and out-of-the-money options.

- Flexibility: Stochastic volatility models can be adapted to include jumps in prices and volatility, further refining the pricing of derivatives that exhibit sensitivity to sudden market movements.

- Market Consistency: These models facilitate the calibration to market data, ensuring that the pricing of derivatives is consistent with the observed prices of liquid instruments like vanilla options.

While stochastic volatility models provide a robust framework for derivative pricing, their implementation is not without challenges. Calibration to market data can be computationally intensive, requiring sophisticated optimization techniques and high-quality market data. Furthermore, the modeling of correlation and the choice of parameters demand careful analysis to avoid mispricing and ensure model stability.

The application of stochastic volatility models in the pricing of complex derivatives represents a significant advancement in financial modeling. By incorporating the random nature of volatility, these models offer a more nuanced and accurate framework for derivative pricing. The Heston model, with its analytical tractability and ability to be calibrated to market data, exemplifies the strengths of stochastic volatility models. However, the successful deployment of these models hinges on a deep understanding of their intricacies and the judicious handling of computational and calibration challenges.

Structured Products Design and Risk Assessment

The design of structured products is both an art and a science, requiring a deep understanding of financial markets, investment psychology, and mathematical prowess. The process begins with identifying the investment objective, which could range from capital preservation for risk-averse investors to leveraging market movements for risk-takers. The next step involves selecting the right combination of derivatives and underlying assets that can achieve the desired payoff structure. Options, futures, swaps, and bonds commonly serve as the building blocks of structured products.

For instance, a structured product aiming to offer capital protection might combine a zero-coupon bond, ensuring the return of principal at maturity, with a call option on a stock index to provide exposure to equity markets. This design leverages the safety of bonds and the growth potential of equities, embodying the dual objectives of protection and participation.

Risk assessment in structured products is a complex endeavor, compounded by their bespoke nature and the interplay of embedded derivatives. The primary risks include market risk, credit risk, liquidity risk, and operational risk. Market risk pertains to fluctuations in the value of underlying assets affecting the product's return. Credit risk involves the possibility of financial loss due to the issuer's default. Liquidity risk arises from the difficulty in selling the product without significant price concessions. Operational risk refers to losses resulting from inadequate internal processes, people, or systems.

Quantitative models play a pivotal role in assessing these risks. For market risk, stochastic models, akin to those discussed in previous sections, evaluate the potential variations in returns under different market conditions. Credit risk assessment requires models that can gauge the creditworthiness of the issuer and the likelihood of default. Liquidity risk assessment involves analyzing the product's market depth and the impact of large trades on its pricing. Operational risk, while more qualitative, necessitates a thorough review of the issuer's operational capabilities and risk management practices.

Given the complexity of structured products and the risks involved, transparency and investor understanding are paramount. Issuers must provide clear, comprehensive documentation detailing the product's structure, underlying components, and risk factors. Financial simulations that illustrate possible outcomes under various market scenarios can aid investors in grasitating the risks and rewards associated with the product.

Education plays a crucial role in bridging the knowledge gap. By fostering a deeper understanding of how structured products work, their potential benefits, and inherent risks, investors can make more informed decisions aligned with their investment goals and risk tolerance.

The design and risk assessment of structured products embody the confluence of financial innovation and rigorous analysis. As these instruments evolve to meet changing market demands and investor preferences, the principles of careful design, thorough risk assessment, and transparency remain the bedrock of creating structured products that can offer value while managing the inherent risks. As we venture further into quantitative finance, the lessons learned here will continue to inform the development of new financial products and strategies, perpetually pushing the boundaries of what is possible in the financial markets.

The Future of Quantitative Finance

The integration of AI and machine learning into quantitative finance is creating unprecedented opportunities for innovation. These technologies have the potential to enhance predictive analytics, improve risk management, and unlock new strategies for trading and investment. For instance, deep learning algorithms can analyze vast datasets to identify patterns and trends that are imperceptible to the human eye, offering more accurate market predictions and investment insights.

Moreover, AI-driven sentiment analysis tools are revolutionizing how financial markets react to news and social media, enabling traders to anticipate market movements based on public sentiment. As these technologies mature, their capacity to augment human decision-making and automate complex processes will become a cornerstone of quantitative finance, leading to more efficient and dynamic financial markets.

Blockchain and distributed ledger technology are poised to redefine the infrastructure of financial markets. By enabling secure, transparent, and tamper-proof transactions, blockchain technology offers a solution to many of the inefficiencies and trust issues that plague current financial systems. Smart contracts, which automatically execute transactions when predefined conditions are met, could automate many aspects of trading and settlement, reducing costs and eliminating intermediaries.

Furthermore, blockchain technology facilitates the creation of decentralized finance (DeFi) platforms, which provide a wide array of financial services, from lending and borrowing to insurance and asset management, without the need for traditional financial institutions. As blockchain technology continues to evolve, its potential to disrupt the financial industry and create more open, accessible, and equitable financial systems is immense.

The rapidly changing landscape of quantitative finance demands a new set of skills and tools. The future quant must be adept not only in mathematics and programming but also in leveraging new technologies such as AI, blockchain, and cloud computing. Moreover, the ability to analyze and derive insights from big data will be crucial, as data becomes increasingly central to financial decision-making.

Continuous learning and adaptability will be the hallmarks of successful finance professionals in this new era. As traditional financial models and strategies are challenged by technological advancements, quants must remain at the forefront of research and innovation, constantly acquiring new knowledge and skills to stay relevant.

The future of quantitative finance is a fusion of technology, data, and innovation. As we venture into this new era, the possibilities are as vast as our imagination and capacity to innovate. The integration of AI and blockchain technology into financial systems heralds a future where markets are more efficient, transparent, and inclusive. However, navigating this future requires a new breed of finance professionals—ones who are not only technically proficient but also adaptable, innovative, and lifelong learners. The journey into the future of quantitative finance is an exciting opportunity to redefine the boundaries of what is possible in the world of finance, ushering in a new age of financial innovation and opportunity.

Emerging Trends in Quantitative Finance and Technology's Role

One of the most electrifying prospects in quantitative finance is the advent of quantum computing. With its prodigious potential to process complex calculations at velocities unfathomable to traditional computers, quantum computing stands as a beacon of hope for solving some of finance's most intractable problems. From optimizing asset allocation models to recalibrating risk assessment frameworks, quantum computing could dramatically enhance the accuracy and speed of quantitative analysis, offering a profound competitive edge.

While AI and machine learning have already made significant inroads into financial markets, their future trajectory points towards even more transformative applications. The next frontier involves moving beyond mere predictive analytics to prescriptive analytics—where AI not only forecasts market trends but also recommends optimal strategies. Furthermore, unsupervised learning algorithms are poised to uncover hidden patterns in market data, revealing insights that could pave the way for groundbreaking trading strategies.

As technology evolves, so does its ability to generate, collect, and process vast amounts of data. Big data, characterized by its volume, velocity, and variety, is becoming the lifeblood of quantitative finance. By harnessing big data, quants can achieve a granular understanding of market dynamics, sentiment analysis, and customer behavior. Moreover, the integration of big data with AI and machine learning is creating sophisticated models that are more nuanced, dynamic, and predictive.

The FinTech revolution, bolstered by developments in blockchain and cryptocurrency, is dramatically altering the financial services landscape. DeFi, or decentralized finance, emerges as a paradigm shift, challenging traditional centralized financial systems with its peer-to-peer networks. DeFi platforms, utilizing blockchain technology, are introducing innovative financial instruments, enhancing transparency, and reducing counterparty risks. This democratization of finance, facilitated by technology, is making financial services more accessible, efficient, and secure.

An emerging trend that marries technology with finance is the burgeoning field of sustainable finance. Leveraging technologies such as AI, IoT (Internet of Things), and blockchain, sustainable finance focuses on directing investments towards environmental, social, and governance (ESG) initiatives. By utilizing quantitative models to assess ESG impacts and risks, technology is playing a crucial role in promoting responsible investing and fostering a sustainable future.

As we peer into the horizon of quantitative finance, it is evident that technology acts not just as a catalyst but as a revolutionary force, driving the field towards uncharted territories. The synergy between quantitative finance and technology is birthing a new era characterized by efficiency, innovation, and inclusivity. However, navigating this evolving landscape requires a fusion of quantitative prowess, technological fluency, and an unyielding commitment to continuous learning. The future of quantitative finance, thus, is not merely an extension of its past but a renaissance, promising a realm of possibilities hitherto unimagined.

The Potential of Blockchain and Distributed Ledger Technology in Finance

blockchain technology is a type of distributed ledger, a decentralized database that is shared, replicated, and synchronized among the members of a network. DLT encompasses blockchain and other similar technologies, all characterized by their lack of a central authority and their reliance on consensus mechanisms to validate transactions. These characteristics not only bolster security and integrity but also facilitate a transparent and immutable record of transactions.

The advent of blockchain technology has paved the way for a myriad of applications within the financial sector, each promising to disrupt traditional practices:

1. Smart Contracts: Self-executing contracts with the terms of the agreement directly written into lines of code. These contracts automatically enforce and execute the terms of agreements without the need for intermediaries, thereby streamlining complex financial transactions and reducing costs.

2. Cross-Border Payments: Blockchain facilitates faster and more cost-effective cross-border payments by eliminating

the need for intermediaries and reducing transaction fees. This capability can revolutionize international trade and remittance markets, which have long been burdened by high costs and inefficiencies.

3. Tokenization of Assets: Blockchain enables the tokenization of real-world assets, such as real estate, art, or commodities, allowing them to be bought, sold, and traded more easily and efficiently on digital platforms. This process democratizes access to investment opportunities and enhances liquidity in markets that were previously inaccessible to many investors.

4. Decentralized Finance (DeFi): DeFi uses blockchain and DLT to create a financial system independent of traditional banks and financial institutions. By leveraging smart contracts and decentralized applications (DApps), DeFi platforms offer a wide range of financial services, including lending, borrowing, and earning interest, without the need for intermediaries.

5. Regulatory Compliance and Transparency: Blockchain can significantly enhance regulatory compliance and transparency in the financial sector. By providing an immutable and transparent record of transactions, it enables more efficient auditing processes, fraud detection, and adherence to anti-money laundering (AML) and know-your-customer (KYC) regulations.

Despite its potential, the integration of blockchain and DLT into the financial sector is not without challenges. Scalability, regulatory uncertainty, and concerns regarding privacy and security are among the hurdles that must be overcome. However, ongoing advancements in technology, coupled with a collaborative approach between innovators, regulators, and industry stakeholders, are paving the way for the realization of blockchain's full potential.

Blockchain and distributed ledger technology hold the promise of radically transforming the finance sector by enhancing efficiency, transparency, and security while reducing costs and democratizing access to financial services. As these technologies continue to evolve and mature, their integration into the financial ecosystem will likely redefine the paradigms of global finance, heralding a new era of innovation, inclusion, and economic empowerment. The journey ahead for blockchain and DLT in finance is not merely about technological adoption but about reimagining and reshaping the financial landscape for the betterment of society.

Adapting to a Changing Financial Landscape: Skills and Tools for the Future Quant

The modern quant must be a polymath, equipped with a diverse skill set that spans various disciplines:

1. Advanced Mathematical Proficiency: quantitative finance lies complex mathematical modeling. A deep understanding of calculus, linear algebra, probability, and statistics is indispensable. The ability to develop and manipulate sophisticated models enables quants to predict market movements and devise effective trading strategies.

2. Computational Expertise: Proficiency in programming languages such as Python, R, and C++ is crucial. The modern quant must adeptly handle large datasets, perform simulations, and implement algorithms. Python, in particular, has emerged as the lingua franca of quantitative finance, given

its rich ecosystem of libraries like NumPy, pandas, and SciPy.

3. Machine Learning and AI Knowledge: With the advent of big data, quants must harness machine learning and AI to uncover patterns and insights from vast datasets that traditional models might overlook. Understanding neural networks, decision trees, and clustering techniques is becoming increasingly important in predicting financial markets' behavior.

4. Blockchain and Cryptocurrency Acumen: As blockchain technology promises to revolutionize financial transactions, a solid grasp of its workings and implications for cryptocurrencies and beyond is essential. Quants should familiarize themselves with smart contracts, tokenization, and the mechanics of various blockchain platforms.

5. Financial Acumen: Beyond technical skills, a thorough understanding of financial theories, instruments, and markets is essential. Quants must navigate complex financial landscapes, understanding the nuances of derivatives, fixed income, equities, and risk management.

To apply these skills effectively, quants must utilize a suite of cutting-edge tools:

1. Quantitative Analysis Software: Platforms like MATLAB, SAS, and QuantLib offer powerful environments for quantitative analysis, allowing for modeling, simulation, and optimization.

2. Data Visualization and Analysis Tools: Tools like Tableau, Power BI, and matplotlib in Python help quants transform

complex data sets into intuitive, actionable insights.

3. Cloud Computing and Big Data Platforms: Amazon Web Services (AWS), Google Cloud Platform (GCP), and Apache Hadoop enable quants to process and analyze big data sets efficiently, leveraging cloud computing's scalability and power.

4. Blockchain Development Platforms: Ethereum, Hyperledger, and other blockchain platforms allow quants to experiment with decentralized applications and smart contracts, exploring their potential in financial contexts.

5. Integrated Development Environments (IDEs): PyCharm, RStudio, and Jupyter Notebooks are essential for coding, offering robust environments for writing, testing, and debugging code.

As the financial landscape continues to evolve, so too will the role of the quant. By mastering a diverse set of skills and leveraging advanced tools, future quants can drive innovation, optimize strategies, and contribute to the financial sector's resilience and growth. The journey ahead is both challenging and exciting, demanding a commitment to continuous learning and an openness to exploring new frontiers in quantitative finance.

The financial landscape of tomorrow will be shaped by those who are not only adept at modeling and analysis but who can also anticipate changes, adapt swiftly, and embrace the convergence of finance with cutting-edge technology. As such, the future quant will not only be a mathematician or a programmer but a visionary capable of leveraging the full spectrum of available tools and skills to redefine the boundaries of what's possible in finance.

ADDITIONAL RESOURCES

Books

1. "Python for Finance: Mastering Data-Driven Finance" by Yves Hilpisch - This book offers a comprehensive exploration of using Python for complex financial analyses and algorithmic trading, making it a great resource for readers interested in building on their Python skills.

2. "Quantitative Risk Management: Concepts, Techniques, and Tools" by Alexander J. McNeil, Rüdiger Frey, and Paul Embrechts - For readers interested in risk management aspects of trading strategies, this book provides advanced quantitative methods and models.

3. "Options, Futures, and Other Derivatives" by John C. Hull - A seminal work in finance that covers the theoretical underpinnings and practical applications of derivatives trading, beneficial for understanding the market instruments involved in stochastic volatility modeling.

4. "The Volatility Surface: A Practitioner's Guide" by Jim Gatheral - An essential read for those looking to deepen their understanding of volatility modeling from a practitioner's standpoint.

5. "Machine Learning for Algorithmic Trading" by Stefan Jansen - Offers insights into the use of machine learning in trading, including feature engineering and strategy optimization, which could be of interest for applying more sophisticated techniques in stochastic volatility models.

Articles & Journals

- The Journal of Computational Finance - This peer-reviewed journal publishes high-quality research on computational finance models, including stochastic volatility. It's an excellent source for staying updated with the latest advancements.

- ArXiv (Quantitative Finance section) - A repository of pre-print papers where researchers often share their work before formal publication. It's a treasure trove for cutting-edge research on stochastic volatility and trading algorithms.

Websites & Blogs

- QuantStart (https://www.quantstart.com/) - Offers articles, tutorials, and guides on quantitative finance, algorithmic trading, and Python programming. It's a great learning resource for practical and theoretical concepts.

- Quantpedia (https://quantpedia.com/) - Known as "The Encyclopedia of Quantitative Trading Strategies," this website catalogs numerous trading strategies and provides research and backtesting results.

Organizations

- CFA Institute - The CFA Program covers many aspects of quantitative finance, including derivatives and portfolio management, which could further enhance a reader's understanding of the financial markets' complexities.

- Global Association of Risk Professionals (GARP) - Offers the Financial Risk Manager (FRM) designation, recognized globally and focusing on risk management in finance, providing deep insights into managing volatility and market risk.

Tools & Software

- QuantLib - A free/open-source library for quantitative finance, providing tools for modeling, trading, and risk management in complex financial instruments.

- RiskMetrics - While technically a product suite provided by MSCI for risk assessment, the methodologies and models it employs for market risk, including stochastic volatility modeling, can be educational.

- Trading platforms with API access like Interactive Brokers or Alpaca - They provide a practical way to implement and test trading strategies developed in Python in real-time market conditions.

Diversifying your study and practice through these resources can significantly deepen your understanding of stochastic volatility modeling and enhance your skills in applying these concepts in real-world trading strategies.

STOCHASTIC VOLATILITY QUICK REFERENCE GUIDE

1. Introduction to Stochastic Volatility

Definition

Stochastic volatility models represent a sophisticated approach to understanding the complexities of financial markets. Unlike traditional models that assume a constant volatility, stochastic volatility models recognize that the volatility of financial assets is itself a random process, subject to change over time. These models are built on the premise that the level of uncertainty or risk associated with an asset's returns does not remain static but fluctuates due to a myriad of market factors. Consequently, they incorporate volatility as a variable that evolves according to its stochastic process, allowing for a more accurate reflection of market behaviors.

Importance

The concept of stochastic volatility is fundamental in several key areas of finance, notably in the pricing of derivatives, risk management, and market analysis. One of its critical contributions is its ability to capture the leptokurtic nature of asset returns. Leptokurtosis refers to the observation that financial return distributions tend to have fatter tails than the normal distribution suggests. This means that extreme returns, whether gains or losses, are more common than traditional models would predict. Stochastic volatility models account for this anomaly, offering a more realistic portrayal of risk.

Additionally, these models address the phenomenon of volatility clustering, where periods of high volatility are followed by more high volatility days, and low volatility days tend to cluster as well. This pattern, observed in financial markets, contradicts the constant volatility assumption and highlights the need for a dynamic approach to volatility modeling.

In derivative pricing, stochastic volatility models provide a crucial framework for understanding options and other financial instruments whose value derives from the underlying asset's price volatility. They allow for more accurate pricing strategies that consider the variable nature of volatility, enhancing market efficiency and the fair valuation of derivatives.

In risk management, recognizing the stochastic nature of volatility enables corporations and financial institutions to better anticipate potential market shifts and adjust their portfolios accordingly. This dynamic understanding of risk helps in devising more effective hedging strategies against market volatility.

Moreover, in conducting financial market analysis, these models facilitate a deeper understanding of market mechanisms, investor behavior, and the potential impact of macroeconomic factors on market volatility. By acknowledging the stochastic properties of volatility, analysts and investors can make more informed decisions, recognizing the inherent uncertainties and the possibilities of sudden market movements.

In essence, stochastic volatility models are indispensable in today's financial landscape, offering a nuanced and comprehensive approach to understanding and navigating the complexities of the markets.

2. Basic Concepts

Volatility

Volatility represents the degree of variation of a trading price series over time, measured by the standard deviation of logarithmic returns. In simpler terms, it is a metric that reflects the rate at which the price of a financial asset increases or decreases for a given set of returns. Volatility is a critical factor in the financial markets, as it indicates the risk or uncertainty related to the change in an asset's value.

Historical vs. Implied Volatility

- **Historical Volatility (Statistical Volatility):** This type of volatility is calculated by analyzing the past market prices of an asset over a specific period. It gives investors and analysts an idea of how much the asset's price has fluctuated in the past. Historical volatility is backward-looking and is used primarily for forecasting future volatility or for model calibration.

- **Implied Volatility:** Unlike historical volatility, implied volatility looks forward, derived from the market price of a derivative, most commonly options. It represents the market's expectation of the future volatility of the underlying asset's price over the life of the option. Implied volatility is a crucial component in options pricing models, as it helps estimate the likelihood of reaching a specific price at expiry. It changes with market sentiment, making it a dynamic and forward-looking measure of market risk perception.

Volatility Clustering

Volatility clustering is a phenomenon observed in financial

markets where periods of high volatility are followed by more high volatility periods, and low volatility periods tend to follow other low volatility periods. This pattern suggests that volatility is not random but exhibits persistence over time. It contradicts models based on constant volatility and underlines the necessity for models that can adapt to changing market conditions, such as stochastic volatility models. Volatility clustering is a key feature that stochastic volatility models aim to capture, allowing them to provide a more accurate representation of real-world financial market behavior.

Understanding these basic concepts is essential for grasping the complexity and dynamism of financial markets. These concepts lay the foundation for exploring more advanced topics in stochastic volatility modeling, which offer sophisticated tools for modeling financial market phenomena.

3. Key Models of Stochastic Volatility

Stochastic volatility models are central to modern financial theory, providing a framework for understanding the dynamic nature of market volatility. These models vary in complexity and application but share the common goal of more accurately capturing the unpredictable behavior of asset prices. Here are some of the most significant stochastic volatility models:

Heston Model

The Heston model, introduced by Steven Heston in 1993, is one of the most widely used stochastic volatility models. It characterizes the volatility of an asset as a stochastic process, allowing for a more accurate depiction of market dynamics. The model assumes that volatility follows a mean-reverting square root process, which means that it tends to return to a long-term average over time. This feature captures the observed volatility clustering in financial markets. The Heston model is particularly popular for pricing European options, as it can produce closed-form solutions for option prices, making it computationally efficient.

SABR Volatility Model

The Stochastic Alpha, Beta, Rho (SABR) model is another prominent stochastic volatility model used primarily to account for the implied volatility smile in derivatives markets. The SABR model describes two stochastic processes: one for the asset price and another for the volatility. It is highly flexible, allowing for the adjustment of parameters to fit various market conditions. This model is especially useful in the fixed income market, where it is employed to price interest rate derivatives.

GARCH Model

While not purely a stochastic volatility model, the Generalized Autoregressive Conditional Heteroskedasticity (GARCH) model is crucial for understanding volatility dynamics. Introduced by Tim Bollerslev in 1986, the GARCH model is an extension of the Autoregressive Conditional Heteroskedasticity (ARCH) model developed by Robert Engle. It models the variance of the current period as a function of the previous periods' variances and squared returns, capturing the volatility clustering phenomenon. GARCH models are extensively used in risk management and financial econometrics for forecasting future volatility based on past data.

Mathematical Foundations

The mathematical underpinning of these models involves stochastic differential equations (SDEs), which describe the evolution of processes that are subject to randomness. Key concepts include Wiener processes (or Brownian motion), which model the random movement part of the SDE, and Itô's Lemma, a fundamental theorem for calculating the differential of a function of a stochastic process. Understanding these mathematical concepts is essential for working with stochastic volatility models, as they provide the tools for describing and solving the models' equations.

These models have transformed financial economics by offering more nuanced ways to understand, measure, and predict volatility. Each model has its strengths and applications, from option pricing to risk management, highlighting the importance of stochastic volatility in contemporary finance.

4. Mathematical Foundations

Stochastic Differential Equations (SDEs)

Stochastic volatility models are deeply rooted in the mathematical framework of stochastic differential equations (SDEs). SDEs are equations that describe how the value of a variable changes over time in a context where those changes are influenced by random variables. These equations are crucial for modeling the unpredictable movements of financial markets and the dynamic nature of volatility. A typical SDE includes a deterministic part, which could follow a simple linear trend, and a stochastic part, which introduces randomness into the model through a Wiener process or Brownian motion.

Wiener Process and Brownian Motion

The Wiener process, also known as Brownian motion, is a continuous-time stochastic process that is central to the theory of stochastic processes. It models the random movement of particles suspended in a fluid, which is analogous to the random fluctuations seen in financial markets. In the context of stochastic volatility, the Wiener process is used to model the unpredictable changes in volatility and asset prices over time.

Itô's Lemma

Itô's Lemma is a fundamental concept in the calculus of

stochastic processes. It provides a method for finding the differential of a function of a stochastic process, essentially allowing the integration of functions of stochastic processes. This is pivotal for stochastic volatility models, as it enables the derivation of equations that describe the evolution of options prices or the underlying asset in a stochastic environment. Itô's Lemma allows for the translation of complex financial theories into practical models that can be used to price derivatives, assess risk, or perform financial analyses under uncertainty.

Numerical Methods for SDEs

Solving SDEs analytically is often challenging or impossible, particularly for complex models of stochastic volatility. As a result, numerical methods play a critical role in the practical application of these models. Two primary numerical methods used in this context are:

- **Monte Carlo Simulation:** This method involves simulating a large number of paths for the stochastic process and then averaging the results to obtain an estimate for the solution. It is widely used for option pricing and risk assessment, where analytical solutions are not feasible.

- **Finite Difference Methods:** These methods involve discretizing the continuous models into a lattice or grid and then solving the resulting discrete equations. Finite difference methods are particularly useful for solving partial differential equations that arise from SDEs, providing approximate solutions for the prices of complex derivatives.

Understanding these mathematical foundations is crucial for anyone working with stochastic volatility models in finance. They provide the tools necessary to model the uncertainty and dynamics of financial markets, enabling more accurate pricing, hedging, and risk management strategies.

HAYDEN VAN DER POST

5. Applications in Finance

The theoretical insights and mathematical frameworks underpinning stochastic volatility models find practical application across various domains within finance. These models enhance the accuracy of financial analysis, derivative pricing, and risk management strategies by accounting for the dynamic and unpredictable nature of market volatility. Below are key areas where stochastic volatility models are extensively applied:

Option Pricing

Stochastic volatility models are pivotal in the pricing of options and other derivatives. Traditional models like the Black-Scholes-Merton formula assume constant volatility, an oversimplification that can lead to pricing inaccuracies for options with longer maturities or those sensitive to volatility changes. Stochastic volatility models, such as the Heston model, allow the volatility to vary, providing a more realistic framework for pricing derivatives. These models can better accommodate the observed market phenomena such as the volatility smile and skew, leading to more accurate market prices for options.

Risk Management

In the realm of risk management, the ability to forecast and quantify the volatility of assets is essential. Stochastic volatility models contribute significantly to this area by offering a more nuanced understanding of the risks associated with financial assets. They enable the calculation of various risk metrics, such as Value at Risk (VaR) and Conditional Value at Risk (CVaR), under scenarios of changing volatility. This dynamic approach to volatility modeling allows firms to better prepare for potential market shifts and to devise strategies that mitigate their exposure to market risk.

Market Analysis

Stochastic volatility models also play a critical role in market analysis, offering insights into the underlying mechanisms driving market movements. By analyzing the stochastic factors that influence volatility, analysts can gain a deeper understanding of market sentiment, investor behavior, and the impact of macroeconomic events on market dynamics. This understanding can inform investment strategies, guide the allocation of assets, and support the development of predictive models that anticipate future market trends.

Portfolio Optimization

The dynamic nature of volatility captured by stochastic models is crucial for portfolio optimization. Investors and portfolio managers use these models to assess the expected returns and risks associated with different asset allocations, taking into account the changing risk landscape. By incorporating stochastic volatility into their models, they can optimize portfolios in a way that balances the trade-off between risk and return, adapting their investment strategies to volatile market conditions.

Algorithmic Trading

In the context of algorithmic trading, stochastic volatility models are used to develop trading strategies that can adapt to the volatility of the market. Algorithms can be programmed to recognize patterns of volatility clustering and to adjust trading activities based on predictions of future volatility. This allows for more sophisticated trading strategies that can capitalize on volatility-induced market opportunities.

The broad applicability of stochastic volatility models underscores their importance in the field of finance. By providing a more accurate and dynamic representation of market volatility, these models empower professionals to make informed decisions, whether in derivative markets, risk management, portfolio construction, or algorithmic trading. Their continued development and refinement will likely remain a central focus of financial research and practice.

STOCHASTIC VOLATILITY TRADING SCENARIOS

Scenario 1: Trading Options Around Earnings Announcements

Step 1: Identify stocks with upcoming earnings announcements, as these events typically result in increased volatility. **Step 2:** Use a stochastic volatility model to forecast potential changes in implied volatility leading up to the earnings release. **Step 3:** Based on the model's forecast, implement a volatility trading strategy, such as straddles or strangles, to profit from the expected increase in volatility. **Step 4:** Monitor the position closely and adjust or close out based on the actual volatility realized post-earnings announcement.

Scenario 2: Exploiting the Volatility Smile

Step 1: Use market data to identify options with a pronounced volatility smile, indicating discrepancies in implied volatility across strike prices. **Step 2:** Apply a stochastic volatility model to assess whether the observed volatility smile offers arbitrage opportunities or mispriced options. **Step 3:** Construct a trading strategy that exploits this mispricing, such as buying undervalued options and/or selling overvalued options. **Step 4:** Manage the risk of the positions and adjust as necessary based on changes in market conditions and model predictions.

Scenario 3: Sector Rotation Strategy Based on Volatility Clustering

Step 1: Analyze historical volatility data across different sectors to identify patterns of volatility clustering. **Step 2:** Use a stochastic volatility model to predict which sectors are likely to experience increased volatility. **Step 3:** Rotate capital into sectors predicted to have higher volatility by trading sector ETFs or options, betting on the increase in price movements. **Step 4:** Regularly review the model's predictions and adjust the portfolio to optimize exposure to sectors with expected high volatility.

Scenario 4: Hedging Portfolio Risk

Step 1: Assess the current volatility exposure of your investment portfolio using a stochastic volatility model. **Step 2:** Determine the optimal hedging strategy based on the model's volatility forecasts, such as purchasing options or using volatility derivatives like VIX futures. **Step 3:** Implement the hedging strategy to protect the portfolio against downside risk associated with forecasted volatility spikes. **Step 4:** Continuously monitor the hedge's effectiveness and adjust the hedging positions as new volatility forecasts are generated by the model.

Scenario 5: Algorithmic Trading Based on Intraday Volatility Patterns

Step 1: Develop an algorithm that uses stochastic volatility models to analyze intraday volatility patterns. **Step 2:** Configure the algorithm to execute trades based on specific signals that indicate short-term increases in volatility, such as sudden jumps or drops. **Step 3:** Employ risk management techniques within the algorithm to limit potential losses, including setting stop-loss orders and position sizing rules. **Step 4:** Continuously backtest and refine the trading algorithm based on historical data and performance metrics to improve its predictive accuracy and profitability.

PYTHON BASICS FOR FINANCE GUIDE

In this guide, we'll dive into the foundational elements of using Python for financial analysis. By mastering variables, data types, and basic operators, you'll be well-equipped to tackle financial calculations and analyses. Let's start by exploring these fundamental concepts with practical examples.

Variables and Data Types

In Python, variables are used to store information that can be reused throughout your code. For financial calculations, you'll primarily work with the following data types:

- **Integers (int)**: Used for whole numbers, such as counting stocks or days.
- **Floats (float)**: Necessary for representing decimal numbers, crucial for price data, interest rates, and returns.
- **Strings (str)**: Used for text, such as ticker symbols or company names.
- **Booleans (bool)**: Represents True or False values, useful for making decisions based on financial criteria.

Example:

python

Defining variables

```python
stock_price = 150.75  # float
company_name = "Tech Innovations Inc."  # string
market_open = True  # boolean
shares_owned = 100  # int

# Printing variable values
print(f"Company: {company_name}")
print(f"Current Stock Price: ${stock_price}")
print(f"Market Open: {market_open}")
print(f"Shares Owned: {shares_owned}")
```

Operators

Operators are used to perform operations on variables and values. In finance, arithmetic operators are particularly useful for various calculations.

- **Addition (+)**: Calculates the total of values or variables.
- **Subtraction (-)**: Determines the difference between values, such as calculating profit or loss.
- **Multiplication (*)**: Useful for calculating total investment or market cap.
- **Division (/)**: Computes the quotient, essential for finding ratios or per-share metrics.
- **Modulus (%)**: Finds the remainder, can be used for periodic payments or dividends.
- **Exponentiation (**)**: Raises a number to the power of another, useful for compound interest calculations.

Example:

python

```
# Initial investment details
initial_investment = 10000.00  # float
annual_interest_rate = 0.05  # 5% interest rate
years = 5  # int

# Compound interest calculation
# Formula: A = P(1 + r/n)^(nt)
# Assuming interest is compounded annually, n = 1
future_value = initial_investment * (1 + annual_interest_rate/1) ** (1*years)

# Calculating profit
profit = future_value - initial_investment

# Printing results
print(f"Future Value: ${future_value:.2f}")
print(f"Profit after {years} years: ${profit:.2f}")
```

In these examples, we've covered the basics of variables, data types, and operators in Python, demonstrating their application in financial contexts. By understanding these fundamentals, you'll be able to perform a wide range of financial calculations and analyses, setting a strong foundation for more advanced finance-related programming tasks.

DATA HANDLING AND ANALYSIS IN PYTHON FOR FINANCE GUIDE

Data handling and analysis are critical in finance for making informed decisions based on historical data and statistical methods. Python provides powerful libraries like Pandas and NumPy, which are essential tools for financial data analysis. Below, we'll explore how to use these libraries for handling financial datasets.

Pandas for Financial Data Manipulation and Analysis

Pandas is a cornerstone library for data manipulation and analysis in Python, offering data structures and operations for manipulating numerical tables and time series.

Key Features:

- **DataFrame**: A two-dimensional, size-mutable, potentially heterogeneous tabular data structure with labeled axes (rows and columns).

- **Series**: A one-dimensional labeled array capable of holding any data type.

Reading Data: Pandas can read data from multiple sources such as CSV files, Excel spreadsheets, and databases. It's particularly useful for loading historical stock data for analysis.

Example: Loading data from a CSV file containing stock prices.

python

import pandas as pd

```
# Load stock data from a CSV file
file_path = 'path/to/your/stock_data.csv'
stock_data = pd.read_csv(file_path)

# Display the first 5 rows of the dataframe
print(stock_data.head())
```

Manipulating DataFrames: You can perform various data manipulation tasks such as filtering, sorting, and aggregating data.

Example: Calculating the moving average of a stock's price.

python

```
# Calculate the 20-day moving average of the closing price
stock_data['20_day_moving_avg']                        =
stock_data['Close'].rolling(window=20).mean()

# Display the result
print(stock_data[['Date',                        'Close',
'20_day_moving_avg']].head(25))
```

Time-Series Analysis: Pandas is particularly suited for time-series analysis, which is fundamental in financial analysis for forecasting, trend analysis, and investment valuation.

python

```
# Convert the Date column to datetime format and set it as the index
stock_data['Date'] = pd.to_datetime(stock_data['Date'])
```

```
stock_data.set_index('Date', inplace=True)
```

```
# Resample the data to get monthly averages
monthly_data = stock_data.resample('M').mean()
```

```
print(monthly_data.head())
```

NumPy for Numerical Calculations in Finance

NumPy is the foundational package for scientific computing in Python. It provides a high-performance multidimensional array object and tools for working with these arrays.

Key Features:

- **Arrays**: NumPy arrays are more efficient for storing and manipulating data than Python lists.

- **Mathematical Functions**: NumPy offers comprehensive mathematical functions to perform calculations on arrays.

Example: Using NumPy for portfolio optimization calculations.

python

```
import numpy as np
```

```
# Example portfolio: percentages of investment in four assets
portfolio_weights = np.array([0.25, 0.25, 0.25, 0.25])
```

```
# Historical returns of the four assets
asset_returns = np.array([0.12, 0.10, 0.14, 0.09])
```

```
# Calculate the expected portfolio return
portfolio_return = np.dot(portfolio_weights, asset_returns)
```

```
print(f"Expected Portfolio Return: {portfolio_return}")
```

NumPy's efficiency in handling numerical operations makes it invaluable for calculations involving matrices, such as those found in portfolio optimization and risk management.

Together, Pandas and NumPy equip you with the necessary tools for data handling and analysis in finance, from basic data manipulation to complex numerical calculations. Mastery of these libraries will greatly enhance your ability to analyze financial markets and make data-driven investment decisions.

TIME SERIES ANALYSIS IN PYTHON FOR FINANCE GUIDE

Time series analysis is essential in finance for analyzing stock prices, economic indicators, and forecasting future financial trends. Python, with libraries like Pandas and built-in modules like datetime, provides robust tools for working with time series data.

Pandas for Time Series Analysis

Pandas offers powerful time series capabilities that are tailor-made for financial data analysis. Its datetime index and associated features enable easy manipulation of time series data.

Handling Dates and Times: Pandas allows you to work with dates and times seamlessly, converting date columns to datetime objects that facilitate time-based indexing and operations.

Example: Converting a date column to a datetime index.

python

import pandas as pd

Sample data loading

data = {'Date': ['2023-01-01', '2023-01-02', '2023-01-03', '2023-01-04'],

```python
'Close': [100, 101, 102, 103]}
df = pd.DataFrame(data)

# Convert the 'Date' column to datetime format
df['Date'] = pd.to_datetime(df['Date'])

# Set 'Date' as the index
df.set_index('Date', inplace=True)

print(df)
```

Resampling for Different Time Frequencies: Pandas' resampling function is invaluable for aggregating data to a higher or lower frequency, such as converting daily data to monthly data.

Example: Resampling daily closing prices to monthly averages.

python

```python
# Assuming 'df' is a DataFrame with daily data
monthly_avg = df.resample('M').mean()

print(monthly_avg)
```

Rolling Window Calculations: Rolling windows are used for calculating moving averages, a common operation in financial analysis for identifying trends.

Example: Calculating a 7-day rolling average of stock prices.

python

```python
# Calculating the 7-day rolling average
df['7_day_avg'] = df['Close'].rolling(window=7).mean()
```

print(df)

DateTime for Managing Dates and Times

The datetime module in Python provides classes for manipulating dates and times in both simple and complex ways. It's particularly useful for operations like calculating differences between dates or scheduling future financial events.

Working with datetime: You can create datetime objects, which represent points in time, and perform operations on them.

Example: Calculating the number of days until a future event.

python

from datetime import datetime, timedelta

Current date

now = datetime.now()

Future event date

event_date = datetime(2023, 12, 31)

Calculate the difference

days_until_event = (event_date - now).days

print(f"Days until event: {days_until_event}")

Scheduling Financial Events: You can use datetime and timedelta to schedule future financial events, such as dividends payments or option expiries.

Example: Adding days to a current date to find the next

payment date.

python

```python
# Assuming a quarterly payment
next_payment_date = now + timedelta(days=90)


print(f"Next payment date: {next_payment_date.strftime('%Y-%m-%d')}")
```

Combining Pandas for data manipulation and datetime for date and time operations offers a comprehensive toolkit for performing time series analysis in finance. These tools allow you to handle, analyze, and forecast financial time series data effectively, which is crucial for making informed investment decisions.

VISUALIZATION IN PYTHON FOR FINANCE GUIDE

Visualization is a key aspect of financial analysis, providing insights into data that might not be immediately apparent from raw numbers alone. Python offers several libraries for creating informative and attractive visualizations, with Matplotlib and Seaborn being the primary choices for static plots, and Plotly for interactive visualizations.

Matplotlib and Seaborn for Financial Data Visualization

Matplotlib is the foundational visualization library in Python, allowing for a wide range of static, animated, and interactive plots. **Seaborn** is built on top of Matplotlib and provides a high-level interface for drawing attractive and informative statistical graphics.

Line Graphs for Stock Price Trends:

Using Matplotlib to plot stock price trends over time is straightforward and effective for visual analysis.

Example:

python

import matplotlib.pyplot as plt

import pandas as pd

```
# Sample DataFrame with stock prices
data = {'Date': pd.date_range(start='1/1/2023', periods=5, freq='D'),
        'Close': [100, 102, 101, 105, 110]}
df = pd.DataFrame(data)
df['Date'] = pd.to_datetime(df['Date'])
df.set_index('Date', inplace=True)

# Plotting
plt.figure(figsize=(10, 6))
plt.plot(df.index, df['Close'], marker='o', linestyle='-', color='b')
plt.title('Stock Price Trend')
plt.xlabel('Date')
plt.ylabel('Close Price')
plt.grid(True)
plt.show()
```

Histograms for Distributions of Returns:

Seaborn makes it easy to create histograms to analyze the distribution of financial returns, helping identify patterns or outliers.

Example:

python

```
import seaborn as sns

# Assuming 'returns' is a Pandas Series of financial returns
returns = df['Close'].pct_change().dropna()
```

```
sns.histplot(returns, bins=20, kde=True, color='skyblue')
```

plt.title('Distribution of Stock Returns')

plt.xlabel('Returns')

plt.ylabel('Frequency')

plt.show()

Heatmaps for Correlation Matrices:

Correlation matrices can be visualized using Seaborn's heatmap function, providing insights into how different financial variables or assets move in relation to each other.

Example:

python

\# Assuming 'data' is a DataFrame with different asset prices

correlation_matrix = data.corr()


```
sns.heatmap(correlation_matrix,              annot=True,
cmap='coolwarm', linewidths=.5)
```

plt.title('Correlation Matrix of Assets')

plt.show()

Plotly for Interactive Plots

Plotly is a graphing library that makes interactive, publication-quality graphs online. It's particularly useful for creating web-based dashboards and reports.

Interactive Line Graphs for Stock Prices:

Plotly's interactive capabilities allow users to hover over points, zoom in/out, and pan through the chart for a detailed analysis.

Example:

python

import plotly.graph_objs as go

\# Sample data

data = go.Scatter(x=df.index, y=df['Close'])

layout = go.Layout(title='Interactive Stock Price Trend',

xaxis=dict(title='Date'),

yaxis=dict(title='Close Price'))

fig = go.Figure(data=data, layout=layout)

fig.show()

Using Matplotlib and Seaborn for static visualizations provides a solid foundation for most financial analysis needs, while Plotly extends these capabilities into the interactive domain, enhancing the user experience and providing deeper insights. Together, these libraries offer a comprehensive suite for financial data visualization, from basic line charts and histograms to complex interactive plots.

ALGORITHMIC TRADING IN PYTHON

Algorithmic trading leverages computational algorithms to execute trades at high speeds and volumes, based on predefined criteria. Python, with its rich ecosystem of libraries, has become a go-to language for developing and testing these algorithms. Two notable libraries in this space are **Backtrader** for backtesting trading strategies and **ccxt** for interfacing with cryptocurrency exchanges.

Backtrader for Backtesting Trading Strategies

Backtrader is a Python library designed for testing trading strategies against historical data. It's known for its simplicity, flexibility, and extensive documentation, making it accessible for both beginners and experienced traders.

Key Features:

- **Strategy Definition**: Easily define your trading logic in a structured way.
- **Data Feeds**: Support for loading various formats of historical data.
- **Indicators and Analyzers**: Comes with built-in indicators and analyzers, allowing for comprehensive strategy analysis.
- **Visualization**: Integrated with Matplotlib for visualizing strategies and trades.

Example: A simple moving average crossover strategy.

```python
import backtrader as bt

class MovingAverageCrossoverStrategy(bt.Strategy):
    params = (('short_window', 10), ('long_window', 30),)

    def __init__(self):
        self.dataclose = self.datas[0].close
        self.order = None
        self.sma_short = bt.indicators.SimpleMovingAverage(self.datas[0], period=self.params.short_window)
        self.sma_long = bt.indicators.SimpleMovingAverage(self.datas[0], period=self.params.long_window)

    def next(self):
        if self.order:
            return

        if self.sma_short[0] > self.sma_long[0]:
            if not self.position:
                self.order = self.buy()
        elif self.sma_short[0] < self.sma_long[0]:
            if self.position:
                self.order = self.sell()

# Create a cerebro entity
```

```
cerebro = bt.Cerebro()

# Add a strategy
cerebro.addstrategy(MovingAverageCrossoverStrategy)

# Load data
data    =    bt.feeds.YahooFinanceData(dataname='AAPL',
fromdate=datetime(2019, 1, 1),
                    todate=datetime(2020, 12, 31))
cerebro.adddata(data)

# Set initial capital
cerebro.broker.setcash(10000.0)

# Run over everything
cerebro.run()

# Plot the result
cerebro.plot()
```

ccxt for Cryptocurrency Trading

ccxt (CryptoCurrency eXchange Trading Library) is a library that enables connectivity with a variety of cryptocurrency exchanges for trading operations. It supports over 100 cryptocurrency exchange markets, providing a unified way of accessing their APIs.

Key Features:

- **Unified API**: Work with a consistent API for various exchanges.

- **Market Data**: Fetch historical market data for analysis.

- **Trading Operations**: Execute trades, manage orders, and access account balances.

Example: Fetching historical data from an exchange.

python

```python
import ccxt
import pandas as pd

# Initialize the exchange
exchange = ccxt.binance({
    'rateLimit': 1200,
    'enableRateLimit': True,
})

# Fetch historical OHLCV data
symbol = 'BTC/USDT'
timeframe = '1d'
since = exchange.parse8601('2020-01-01T00:00:00Z')

ohlcv = exchange.fetch_ohlcv(symbol, timeframe, since)

# Convert to DataFrame
df = pd.DataFrame(ohlcv, columns=['timestamp', 'open', 'high', 'low', 'close', 'volume'])
df['timestamp'] = pd.to_datetime(df['timestamp'], unit='ms')

print(df.head())
```

Both **Backtrader** and **ccxt** are powerful tools in the domain of algorithmic trading, each serving different stages of the trading strategy lifecycle. Backtrader is ideal for backtesting strategies to ensure their viability before real-world application, while ccxt is perfect for executing trades based on strategies developed and tested with tools like Backtrader. Together, they form a comprehensive toolkit for Python-based algorithmic trading, especially relevant in the rapidly evolving world of cryptocurrencies.

Made in the USA
Las Vegas, NV
01 April 2024

88124283R00184